Frank Lloyd Wright Mid-Century Modern

Frank Lloyd Wright Mid-Century Modern

PHOTOGRAPHS BY ALAN WEINTRAUB | TEXT BY ALAN HESS

with contributions by John Zukowsky and Monica Ramírez-Montagut

RIZZOLI
NEW YORK

For Michael Duté

— AW

For Jonathan, Emma, and family

— AH

First published in the
United States of America in 2007 by
RIZZOLI INTERNATIONAL
PUBLICATIONS, INC.
300 Park Avenue South
New York, NY 10010
www.rizzoliusa.com

ISBN-10: 0-8478-2976-6
ISBN-13: 978-0-8478-2976-7

Library of Congress Control Number:
2007922838

Photography (except when otherwise noted
throughout book) © 2007 Alan Weintraub/
Arcaid@arcaid.co.uk

Text (except as noted below) © 2007 Alan Hess

"Frank Lloyd Wright and World War II,
1939–45" (pp. 40–42) © 2007 John Zukowsky

"Exuberant Fifties, Wright, and the
Guggenheim" (pp. 44–47) © 2007 Monica
Ramírez Montagut

© 2007 Rizzoli International Publications

Front cover: Mrs. Clinton Walker House
Back cover: Goetsch-Winckler House
Endpapers: Llewellyn Wright House
p. 2: Seth Condon Peterson Cottage
pp. 6–7: Raymond Carlson House
pp. 48–49: C. Leigh Stevens House
p. 336: Arch Oboler House

Distributed to the U.S. trade by
Random House, New York

Designed by Zand Gee

Printed and bound in China

2007 2008 2009 2010 2011/ 10 9 8 7 6 5 4 3 2 1

Contents

Mid-Century Houses

Frank Lloyd Wright: Mid-Century Modern

By Alan Hess

**Fallingwater is only the tip
of the iceberg.**

Frank Lloyd Wright's most famous house, perched above a Pennsylvania woodland stream, allowed him to return to the center stage of the architectural world in 1935 after two decades of relative obscurity. During the two remaining decades of his life, he would enjoy fame even more than fortune. More importantly, he was given opportunities to build. Almost overnight, authors, editors, architects, and critics lavished praise on him. Clients arrived from all over the world to commission buildings. His ideas about architecture spread to hundreds of architects. Most pleasing of all to him, Wright could no longer be ignored by friend or foe.

In the twenty-four years until his death in 1959, he would design and build several of the twentieth century's most astonishing buildings. In a period of extraordinary architectural renewal after the dark decade of World War II, Wright more than held his own. Yet for all his success, Wright and the mainstream architecture world slowly diverged in the 1950s. He always reveled in being in the righteous minority. And though the creativity and imagination of many of his designs could not be dismissed, other Wright designs of this period were met with skepticism. Some believed that the bard of Taliesin had gone too far, had succumbed to his ego and the adulation, and lost all discipline. He was too far out. Ultimately Wright's more innovative designs were dismissed or quietly overlooked by critics even as the magnificence of his best

work was accepted. And yet we must be careful not to dismiss the work of such a protean artist.

The designs which made critics uneasy are fields of circles, spirals, cantilevers, saucers, spires, and other perplexing shapes, seen in the Marin County Civic Center, Beth Shalom Synagogue, Grady Gammage Auditorium, Auldbrass, the David Wright House, the Sol Friedman House, and unbuilt designs, including the Donahoe Triptych House and the Huntington Hartford Play Resort. Compared to conventional landmarks of mid-century architecture—the Seagram Building by Mies van der Rohe, the General Motors Technical Center by Eero Saarinen, and even Chandigarh by Le Corbusier—these designs were off the radar. They offered—no, *insisted* on—an entirely new geometry for walls and plans, an aesthetic of opulence rather than simplicity.

Today the variety and freshness of Wright's later architecture remains astonishing. Even the two decades of his Prairie Style at the beginning of the twentieth century—still startling in its re-conception of the American house—could not compete in terms of fertility. While it is true that, during those last busy decades, he often borrowed from unbuilt designs he had developed during his middle decades toiling in the architectural wilderness, the energy and imagination of these designs demand admiration.[1]

For the moment we will confine this reconsideration of Wright's later work to his residential designs. Which of these is the most important? Is it one of the dozens of Usonian houses he designed and built across

America? These modest-sized houses put a new, casual middle-class lifestyle into artful form, melding living room, dining room, and kitchen into a single articulated space. Is it the great custom homes for well-to-do clients? Is Fallingwater greater than Wingspread? Is Auldbrass more expressive of its wetlands environment than the coastal mountains of Eaglefeather? Each of these grand houses is a distinct idea and aesthetic direction, and each design is fully realized. Is it the houses that embodied mid-century prosperity, technology, and confidence in the future? Is it his explorations of cement and asbestos boards ("Cemesto") in modular three-dimensional frames, or his experiments with custom-designed concrete blocks in the Usonian Automatic homes, his use of the common eight-inch-by-sixteen-inch concrete cinder blocks, or his schemes for prefabricated, mass-produced homes? Is it his houses fashioned on circles or curves, or his houses elaborating on triangles and parallelograms, or his houses based on the right angles and grids?

* * *

Part of the fascination of Wright in this period is that his work existed in two entirely separate dimensions: one utterly in tune with the real world advancing around him, and the other in a visionary world (or city), which was his alone.

Opposite page: Jean and Paul Hanna House, (Honeycomb House), Palo Alto, California, 1936

RANCH
Above, top: A. H. Bulbulian House, Rochester, Minnesota, 1947; Middle: Albert Adelman House, Fox Point, Wisconsin,1948; Bottom: Isadore and Lucille Zimmerman House, Manchester, New Hampshire, 1950 (1952)

USONIAN HOUSES
Opposite page, top: John C. Pew House, Shorewood Hills, Wisconsin, 1938; Bottom: Loren B. Pope (Pope-Leighey) House, Falls Church, Virginia, 1939

Wright was fully aware of the changing society around him in the post–World War II era. Despite having grown up in the Gilded Age of horses, buggies, parlors, and domestic servants, his mid-twentieth century houses have open kitchens and unified living areas that functioned well for young families without the servants of his earlier Victorian-era houses. He fully embraced cars, carports, drive-ins, and car-accessible suburban sites, which became essential inspirations for his designs. On the domestic scale he designed TV tables for his houses in full recognition of modern communications, and on urban and regional scale he designed atomic-powered barges as part of the transportation system of Broadacre City.[2] Since he began building in Oak Park, Illinois, in the 1890s, he had been more of a suburban architect than an urban one; and as suburbia became the leading growth area after World War II in the United States, Wright continued to design houses that brilliantly captured the sense of modern family life in touch with nature and accessed by the automobile. He understood his own time with an intimacy that most elite architects shunned. In turn, society fully embraced the eccentric genius with the assured voice of a television prophet, at once chiding and wittily cajoling the nation away from its foolish architectural sins and foibles. He was quoted in newspapers, and magazines heralded him or clucked agreeably at his carefully fashioned eccentricities. Congress listened to his opinions on buildings of national concern, such as the new Air Force Academy to be built in Colorado Springs. Wright in his seventies and eighties was fully engaged with his time.

Wright's firm involvement with the cultural trends of the 1940s and 1950s is evidenced by his complex relationship with the era's most popular and widely built house type: the Ranch house. As the middle-class moved to the suburbs, it was the home of choice: a single-family, gable-roofed, one-story house with open interiors and closely tied to its garden. It could be clothed in traditional Ranch's board and batten walls and roofed in shingles, or it could take on the clean lines of the contemporary Ranch house. Above all it was suburban, emblematic of the demographic tide toward living outside cities, taking advantage of the automobile and newly developed land at the fringes of the traditional city. Wright's suburban Prairie houses, designed decades earlier, were an early prototype of this widely built type, and he continued his own evolution of the ranch house in the 1950s. The Bulbulian House, the Albert Adelman House, the Brown House, the Schaberg House, and the Zimmerman House are all long, sprawling homes on suburban sites, capped with gabled roofs whose eaves spread gracefully beyond the walls. Equally in tune with the times were three suburban tracts for which Wright not only designed homes but also plotted the streets and sites. The Galesburg and Parkwyn tracts outside Kalamazoo, Michigan, are two fragments of Broadacre City that were actually built. On gently rolling, forested acreage, roads follow the natural topography, and each house enjoys its own spacious lawns and its own private views. Wright's houses designed suburbia in the same way that custom and mass-produced home tracts by other architects and developers did in the same era.

But for all his embrace of the technology, social trends, and media, the real world was only an instrument that Wright manipulated to achieve his overriding goal: the building of Broadacre City. He had first conceived of this ideal city in the early 1930s when he was building little. In this design he projected current social trends onto his deeply held philosophical beliefs rooted in

Jefferson, Emerson, Whitman, and Sullivan. He carefully melded the modern technology of the automobile with his deep respect for nature; homes, factories, offices, shops, schools, and civic centers were spread out so that every citizen maintained a close relationship with agrarian culture or untouched nature. Most of Wright's residential and public designs after 1935 fleshed out this vision in architecture; even in the real world, the United States federal government's interstate highway system of the 1950s and commercial merchant builders' mass-produced housing tracts reflected Broadacre City's sleek, suburban, mobile future lifestyle. For Wright, each client who brought the funds and the property for a house was furthering this purpose. Wright had many motivations to build, of course; he was a vain, jealous, and driven man in need of constant affirmation of his greatness. But he was also a visionary rooted in American philosophical tradition. A constant theme of his writings, lectures, and designs was transforming the United States into a modern version of Jefferson's agrarian society that would be dedicated to the worship of Emerson's Nature—and in the image envisioned by Frank Lloyd Wright.

The strength of this vision is still powerfully tangible today. Walk through the door of one of his houses from this period, and you walk into a new realm that is strikingly different. The walls extend out in a geometry different than the world with which we are familiar; the ornament blossoms from seeds more exotic and sumptuous than our contemporary glitz or bling could fathom. You've walked into a small piece of Broadacre City. This is one reason why many of these designs are still controversial.

The tension between Wright's real presence in the mid-twentieth century world and his insistence on building for a world

USONIAN HOUSES
Top, left to right: Ben Rebhuhn House, Great Neck
Estates, New York, 1937; Lloyd Lewis House,
Libertyville, Illinois, 1939; Joseph Euchtman House,
Baltimore, Maryland, 1939; Bottom, left to right:
James B. Christie House; Bernardsville,
New Jersey, 1940; Charles Weltzheimer House,
Oberlin, Ohio, 1947

Opposite page: Edward Serlin House, Pleasantville,
New York, 1949

that pressed beyond its boundaries creates
the fascinating dilemma of the last part of
his career. It also explains why we still have
problems embracing many of his later
designs, even while we continue to embrace
Wright as the ultimate architect. We adore
him as a visionary, but many of us have been
uncomfortable with living with his visions in
the real world. We can take a small dose of
Wright at a time: an occasional visit to the
Guggenheim Museum in New York, or a tour
of his local houses in our cities. Civil
servants and citizens who use his largest
and most public building, Marin County Civic
Center, straddle that dilemma daily. It must
function as a working courthouse,
administration building, library, and jail, but
the long walkways, the open-air corridors,
the demands for expansion, and the

maintenance on a forty-five-year old building
quickly bring the vision down to earth.

* * *

Part of the exotic power of Wright's later
designs is due to the fact that his vision
ultimately lost a culture war of the 1940s and
1950s. Though his ideas influenced suburban
development, today the designs remain
largely outside conventional aesthetics—but
they almost became the dominant
architecture of the mid-century.

Organic architecture surged to the
forefront of American design on the crest of
Wright's designs for Fallingwater, Johnson
Wax Company, the Usonian houses, the
Synagogue, Price Tower, the Guggenheim,
and dozens of houses published nationally
and locally. Around the country, architects

USONIAN HOUSES

Top: Stuart Richardson House, Glen Ridge, New Jersey, 1941; Middle: Theodore Baird House, Amherst, Massachusetts, 1940; Bottom: Chauncey and Johanna Griggs House, Tacoma, Washington, 1946

Opposite, top: Drawing of Arch Obeler House (Eaglefeather), Los Angeles, Califorrnia, 1941; Bottom: Plan of Herbert Johnson House (Wingspread), Wind Point, Wisconsin, 1937

Drawings of Frank Lloyd Wright are Copyright © 2007 The Frank Lloyd Wright Foundation, Taliesin West, Scottsdale, AZ.

who trained at Wright's Taliesin Fellowship established extraordinarily vital and noteworthy careers in the 1940s and 1950s: John Lautner in Los Angeles, Aaron Green in San Francisco, Fay Jones in Arkansas, Alden Dow in Michigan, Mark Mills in Monterey, and others. Other architects (including several large firms) inspired by Wright's ideas also promoted Organic architecture: MacKie and Kamrath in Houston, Alfred Browning Parker in Florida, Paul Schweikher in Chicago, Anshen and Allen in San Francisco, Armét and Davis in Los Angeles, August Sarmiento in St. Louis, Harwell Hamilton Harris in Texas and California, and Bruce Goff in Oklahoma. This wave of inspired designs showed the vitality of Organic Modernism in the face of the dominant International Style Modernism favored by Mies van der Rohe, Walter Gropius, Pietro Belluschi, Skidmore, Owings & Merrill, Welton Becket Associates, and other large firms of the day. In-between these extremes, Eero Saarinen, Minoru Yamasaki, Morris Lapidus, Edward Durell Stone, and William Pereira took organic and expressionist forms seriously enough to create a broad middle ground. This breadth of ideas sparked controversy and debate in both professional and popular magazines. Editor Elizabeth Gordon was a powerful proponent of all things Wrightian in the influential pages of *House Beautiful*, and for a time around 1960 Wright and Organic Modernism seemed poised to become the nation's dominant style.

Perhaps it was Wright's death in April 1959 that reversed the tide; he had been the movement's most successful advocate. Certainly there were powerful forces on the other side. Tastemakers such as New York's Museum of Modern Art, while giving Wright his due in exhibits and publications, militated toward the International Style. One measure of this lack of acceptance can be seen in the career of Phillip Johnson, a curator at MOMA

and a weathervane of Modernism. He never had an Organic phase. Johnson had Miesian, Expressionist, Post Modern and Corporativist phases, but despite his long friendship with Wright he never designed in an organic manner. Likewise social, commercial, and technological forces moved toward a broad-based modularization and mass production that Wright, with his philosophical emphasis on individuality, was not disposed to embrace. Architecture schools also never widely adopted Wright's curriculum, except for the University of Oklahoma under Bruce Goff in the early 1950s and Taliesin.

What was judged and found wanting in its day, however, deserves a closer look today. The fertility of Wright's imagination in this second long chapter of his career is astounding. The forms still provoke, amaze, and appall. The richness of his ornament— almost always growing out of the structure, space, or site—creates a world of wonder that transports us away from the minimalist severity of today's aging avant-garde.

* * *

The twenty-some years from Wright's Imperial Hotel commission in 1913 to the beginning of Fallingwater's design in 1934 were bitter. The grand hotel should have been the foundation of a magnificent career, as the Auditorium Hotel had launched his mentors Adler and Sullivan as major Chicago architects in 1890; instead the years overseas dried up the connections to clients that an architecture practice needed, as his son Lloyd had warned.[3] Broaching the idea of moving to Los Angeles (where his few houses in this period were built) on his return, he instead settled in Spring Green, Wisconsin, just far enough from big clients to discourage them from hiring him. An enervating relationship with Miriam Noel drained more energy. The will and the way to build a successful architecture practice escaped him. The young *wunderkind* of the Prairie years no longer attracted clients.

Still, Wright's creativity did not abandon him. He designed a multi-faceted skyscraper for New York, teepee-like cabins for the snows of Lake Tahoe, and the concrete textile block system he used in the Los Angeles houses of the early 1920s. Habitually (and congenitally) in debt, Wright still found enough clients with enough money and enough daring to keep him going in straitened circumstances—and he had his Japanese prints to sell off when he could no longer ward off the creditors. Olgivanna Lazovich, the new, young wife he married in 1928, inspired Wright to found the Taliesin Fellowship in 1932, which opened the way for the rejuvenation of his career.

By the late 1930s, as he embarked on the final two decades of his life at the heart of America's prosperous and confident mid-century, Wright was well-established once again. And the designs showed it.

Fallingwater was followed by the Johnson Wax headquarters, and a house in Racine, Wisconsin, dubbed Wingspread, for its president, Herbert Johnson. For two Stanford professors he designed an intriguing design based on a honeycomb module—at once more complex and more suggestive than the simple grids that most modern architects were using at the time. Wealthy clients such as Edgar Kaufmann, Herbert Johnson, C. Leigh Stevens, and Arch Oboler gave Wright the freedom of large, well-funded residential designs, and he also worked on small houses for the average family, and designed the first in a long series of so-called Usonian houses for Herbert and Katherine Jacobs. Large public commissions came in and were built: Florida Southern College campus (1938), the Guggenheim Museum (1943). Other large commissions came in and were not built: a spa for Elizabeth Arden, a resort for Huntington Hartford.

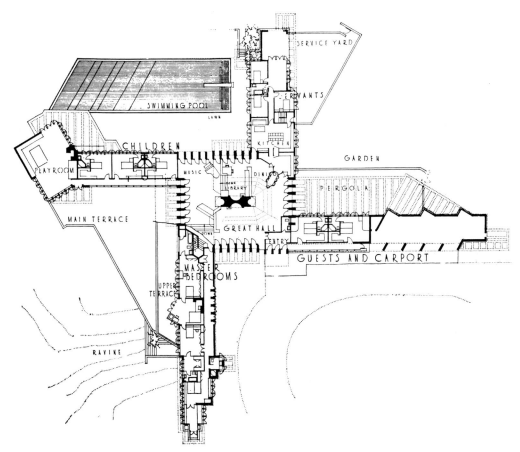

The extraordinary range of shapes, forms, and concepts in these mid-century designs is proof of the resourcefulness of Wright's imagination and the fruitfulness of his concepts. At times he did draw on earlier unbuilt designs, and he often repeated some favored forms, but the variety of forms and solutions shows that he did, more often than not, obey his own stated philosophy that a building form should express the unique nature of a site, a client, a climate, or a structural technology. This was a key aspect of his Organic philosophy.

* * *

The large homes Wright designed for several wealthy clients at the beginning of the second phase of his career display the remarkable variety of solutions and forms which he was capable of producing, even as he approached seventy years of age. Fallingwater (1935), overlooking a woodland waterfall splashing through a Pennsylvania forest, poises its long, astonishingly cantilevered concrete viewing balconies against vertical stone escarpments that echo the wild, rocky setting; Wright distills the environment into a poetic statement. Wingspread (1937) on a flat Wisconsin site

USONIAN HOUSES

Top row, left to right: Carroll Alsop House, Oskaloosa, Iowa, 1947; John Carr House, Glenview, Illinois, 1950; Robert and Elizabeth Muirhead House, Plato Center, Illinois, 1950 (1951)

Middle row, left to right: Seamour and Gerte Shavin House, Chattanooga, Tennessee, 1950; Frank Sander House (Springbough) Stamford, Connecticut, 1952; Ray Brandes House, Issaquah, Washington, 1950

Bottom row, left to right: Alice and Ellis Feiman House, Canton, Ohio, 1954 (1955); Paul and Ida Trier House, Johnston, Iowa, 1956 (1960)

self-consciously ignores the conventions of magnificent pillared facades preferred by most wealthy clients for an utterly unique form: an octagonal dome sits at the center of four wings spiraling out into the landscape. Wright called it the "last of the Prairie houses," and perhaps it is in his reckoning.[4] Certainly the spiral wings recall the layout of the Coonley and other Prairie houses from thirty years before. If we are to accept Wright's appraisal, he leaves the Prairie style's rectilinear arrangement of space behind with this house to explore a realm of triangles and curves in his new career. Like domes since Roman times, Wingspread's dome marks the center of the house and the space, but Wright completely reinvents it in every other conceivable manner. The dome is a stretched octagon pierced with clerestory windows instead of a central oculus; in place of a traditional central cupola an offset observatory connects dome to sky. Inside, the central chimney is ringed by four hearths facing the entry hall, living room, dining, and music areas. Light pours in from above. This residence thoroughly reconfigures all expectations of the traditional house—a theme of Wright's work through the next twenty years. Auldbrass (1938), set in a swampy lowland forest, is a collection of wooden shacks open to the movement of every cooling breeze and perfectly at ease in the humid climate. Its tilting walls seem lazy, almost ramshackle, certainly casual, and are unlike anything else in Wright's work to that time (though he would continue to explore walls that defied the conventions of gravity). Each building of Auldbrass drips with wood ornamental details, highlighting the posts and eaves, that echo the Spanish moss hanging from the trees. A fourth great house should be added to the list: Eaglefeather, for radio and movie producer Arch Oboler. It was never completed, but the pieces that were

completed show another design as distinct as Fallingwater, Wingspread, and Auldbrass. Here the bare mountain peaks on the site looking toward the Pacific are capped with concrete and wood structures and terraces, capturing the treeless, dry, rolling landscape as Fallingwater captured the Pennsylvania forest.

But the fifth great house of this period is probably the most important in terms of Wright's formal exploration: his second home, Taliesin West, in Scottsdale, Arizona. Since 1927 Wright had been regularly visiting the Arizona desert and had camped there yearly with his apprentices. But his decision to adopt the desert as his second home to complement the beloved Taliesin in his native Spring Green, Wisconsin, marks a profound and unequivocal new direction in his work.

From a career standpoint, the move to Arizona was counter-intuitive. When his career was springing back to life in the late 1930s, he might have created a new base in Chicago, or at least Los Angeles. Instead he chose a virtual wilderness, a backwater, where his apprentices had to struggle just to get a clear phone connection to their growing number of clients and building sites. But Wright's intuition led him to explore the colors, the spaces, the materials of the desert. In retrospect, he proved to be ahead of the socio-economic curve. Though few realized it before World War II, Phoenix was to become part of the booming Sunbelt, America's magnet for growth in the mid-century. It was to be suburban, with an ongoing connection to nature. By establishing his foothold in this proto-suburb, Wright was to cement his influence on many of the real world growth trends in the second half of the century.

Like his other homes in Oak Park and Spring Green, Taliesin West was a laboratory for design. As his own client he could explore his own aesthetic desires, and he

MULTIPLE HOUSING CONCEPTS
Top: Suntop Homes, Ardmore, Pennsylvania, 1938;
Middle: Thomas Keys House, Rochester,
Minnesota, 1951

PARKWYN VILLAGE
Bottom: Robert Levin House, Kalamazoo, Michigan,
1948

Opposite, top: Broadacre City drawing, 1958;
Bottom: Baghdad Cultural Center drawing, 1957

could build, tear down, revise, and rebuild to his heart's desire—with the help of on-site apprentices. In the shadow of a mountain peak, Taliesin West sprawled across the desert and allowed the architect to explore unusual angles on a larger scale with a tightly composed set of varied forms, with long bold sweeping lines, punctuated by ever-changing patterns, textures, and colors. He had worked with the hexagon module at the Hanna House (1936). In the Wall House (1941) he first used the triangle and parallelogram as an organizing principle to determine the placement of walls, doors, and windows. Now he used these oblique and acute geometries to create and unite a collection of buildings over a large site. Some of the structure became landmark prows jutting into the desert vista due to its geometries; this allowed long promenades to stretch out into the landscape, their endpoints accented by other balancing forms. Courtyards and compounds grew naturally as Wright played with these geometries. These lessons would be repeated in many houses over the next two decades.

The desert suggested new materials, colors, and textures to Wright, too. Concrete had always interested him; now he took it in a new direction inspired by the sand and vast vistas. The monolithic concrete he had explored in the neat planes of Unity Temple in 1904 was transformed into adventurous, raw collages of concrete and desert stone. In the early 1920s he had impressed gorgeous abstract designs onto the textile block of the Los Angeles houses to create rich textures catching the strong sunlight; now he relied on the rough natural texture of desert stone, pulled directly from the sand and wrestled into concrete formwork, for visual interest. Instead of painting colorful friezes (as he had in the Prairie years) or adding colored art glass to windows, he let the rusts, reds,

tans, and oranges of the natural desert speak for themselves in his houses. Even the concrete floors were left exposed, though tinted with complementary color.

THE BROADACRE HOUSES

Wright's residential designs in the 1940s and 1950s ranged widely. A series of drawings of Broadacre City by Wright and his apprentices in the 1950s show his ultimate vision of a city in nature. Dotted among the hills and valleys of this rolling landscape—a landscape not identifiably desert or plain—are the buildings of both Wright's career and of his imagination. The houses in these drawings include some of Wright's most fantastic: the Play Resort for Huntington Hartford juts out as a pyramidal outcropping, with its saucer-shaped rooms cantilevered out in an odd sculptural composition. That extraordinary structure was never built, but Wright was able to build, in real space and time, several of the ultramodern houses that populated his psyche.

The most numerous designs belong to the Usonian series, which bear a genetic similarity. Though modern, they were exercises in easy, simplified construction and practical living. In other designs Wright allowed himself to push far beyond the conventional boundaries of form and space, pursuing flights of architectural fancy in the same way as his apprentice John Lautner and his colleague Bruce Goff.

The innovative Usonian designs were filled with ideas: basement-less houses were built on concrete slabs, and pipes running through the slab were filled with heated water, which radiated an even heat throughout the house. Single-walled board and batten walls replaced wood stud and plaster or brick wall construction. The small efficient kitchen was open to the dining room, which was open to the living room. Built-in couches eliminated the need for most furniture and created a unified space. An open carport was elegantly integrated into the roofline of the house, right next to the front door; the car was not hidden in a dark storage shed but became part of the design of the house itself. Warm brick and polished natural wood usually formed the materials inside and out.

The Usonians were not, however, mass-produced or mass-manufactured houses, like those that would spread across suburbia in the 1950s. Though they shared general forms, each house was custom designed for the client and site—often by Taliesin Fellow John Howe under Wright's supervision. The open plan and structure were easy enough for some homeowners to build themselves —these clients were Wright's ideal for the designs. When Wright attempted to design a true pre-fabricated house for developer Marshall Erdman in 1956, the constraints of the manufacturing system produced a design much less flexible and innovative than the Usonian houses.

Wright did develop other simpler, repeatable house designs besides the Usonian model. Some involved construction techniques that he applied; others involved a model type.

Two construction methods he found intriguing resulted in the Cemesto and the Usonian Automatic houses. The former was a panel system of cement and asbestos framed in wood. The resulting houses (see the Carlson and Penfield houses) reveal the distinct rectilinear geometry of the prefabricated panels: the form follows the structure, but with the rich interplay of interlocking one- and two-story spaces we expect of Wright. The Usonian Automatic houses followed from Wright's long interest in concrete blocks. In 1951 he developed a system of one-by-two-foot blocks fabricated on-site by a custom-designed machine. The blocks varied: some were solid coffered

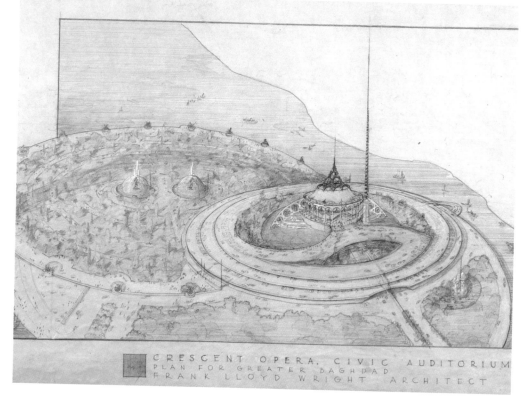

CRESCENT OPERA, CIVIC AUDITORIUM
PLAN FOR GREATER BAGHDAD
FRANK LLOYD WRIGHT ARCHITECT

GALESBURG COUNTRY HOMES
Top row, left to right: Samuel Eppstein House, Galesburg, Michigan, 1948; David and Christine Weisblat House, Galesburg, Michigan, 1948; Eric and Pat Pratt House, Galesburg, Michigan, 1948

USONIAN AUTOMATIC
Bottom row, left to right: Benjamin Adelman House, Phoenix, Arizona, 1951; Toufic Kalil House, Manchester, New Hampshire, 1955

USONIAN HOUSES
Opposite: John and Catherine Christian House West Lafayette, Indiana, 1954 (1956)

blocks; some blocks framed glass; and some were for ceilings, creating a full three-dimensional structure and space. In examples like the Benjamin Adelman, Turkel, and Kalil houses, the textural richness of the coffered blocks helps to counter the hardness of the concrete, but the obsessive geometry of the beehive-like interiors emphasize the faults of Wright's insistence on total design: too much unity can be a bad thing.

Wright designed another prototype house plan in 1938 for a cooperative development in Madison Heights, Michigan. The approaching war stalled that community, but Wright saved the design and built one example as a custom home, the 1950 Keys House in Minnesota. Here a gabled roof, not the Usonian's flat roof, topped the house. The main room (combining living room,

kitchen, and dining area) is one open space defined by rectangular blocks holding utility spaces and supporting the roof. This prototype was designed as part of a neighborhood of similar houses, unlike the Usonians. Where the Usonians turned a blank wall to the street and a wall of tall glass doors to the backyard, this prototype faced outdoor patios on both sides of the house through glass walls. Earthen berms that rise half way up the concrete block walls distinguish the design; high windows are tucked beneath the gabled roof's wide eaves. The design is simple, logical, and efficient. It also shows how Wright's restless imagination was never satisfied with one solution, and was always searching for new ways to solve problems and express the concept of home.

VARIED GEOMETRIES, Top: Charles L. Manson House, Wausau, Wisconsin, 1938; Middle: Andrew Armstrong House, Ogden Dunes, Indiana, 1939; Bottom: James and Dolores Edwards House, Okemos, Michigan, 1949

CEMESTO SYSTEMS, Opposite page, top: Louis Penfield House, Willoughby Hills, Ohio, 1952

ORGANIC MODERNISM, Opposite page, bottom: Huntington Hartford Play Resort (1947)

Drawings of Frank Lloyd Wright are Copyright © 2007 The Frank Lloyd Wright Foundation, Taliesin West, Scottsdale, AZ.

In their way the Usonian houses were explorations of the future as vivid as anything H. G. Wells or Arthur Clarke imagined in writing or cinema. Repeatability and modularity gave the Usonians' structure and shapes a certain discipline. But Wright did not shy away from daring and extravagant design in order to promote his vision of Broadacre City. These houses were often phantasms, extreme concepts that leapt forward into an imaginative peaceable kingdom where man and machine laid down in the garden. Wright's ideal world, where whirligigs shaped like odd dragonflies or milkweed seeds transported people hither and yon, paralleled the scenes of science-fiction movies of the era. Believing fervently that architecture could resolve the conflicts of society, technology, and nature, Wright's futurism was both utopian and optimistic.

With his designs Wright often anticipated the future. The famous Robie House was likened to a steamship, the thrilling symbol of advanced technology in 1906. The Gilmore House (1908) was called the Airplane House only five years after the Wright brothers first flew. But after 1950 this projection of the future was too romantic for most of the serious tastemakers in the architectural profession to embrace. Wright's bold—some said indulgent and excessive— search for new forms sometimes created strange and unworldly shapes that many could not take seriously. The same response greeted Oscar Niemeyer's odd curvilinear and surreal architecture in Brazil, culminating with his striking stage-set national capitol of Brasilia in 1957. These mystical and mythical aspects of ostensibly rational and functional Modern architecture made mainstream Modernists distinctly uneasy. For the architecture profession enamored with the "articulated skeleton" (in Lewis Mumford's words) of the International Style, this dual

rejection of convention by a powerful dowager king and a renegade prince of the realm was unnerving.[5]

Wright's tendency to use exotic forms and opulent ornament in his later years put him at odds with the architectural establishment of the 1950s. Part of this may be chalked up to Wright's contrarian attitudes, which often served him well, and to his romantic nineteenth-century sensibility. But when he was invited by the King of Iraq to visit and design an opera house and auditorium for Baghdad in 1957, the "Thousand-and-One-Nights" character of these later designs, draped with gold-anodized loops and architectural jewelry, only confirmed Wright's decadence in the eyes of his critics.[6]

Many critics felt that the Old Man had gone too far, that he had lost the sure hand and aesthetic judgment that created the Prairie houses and Fallingwater. Tales of the almost medieval, lordly manor life of Mr. and Mrs. Wright and their acolytes at Taliesin only encouraged this criticism. Wright himself was beyond caring about what they thought, but this reaction damaged the effort to establish Organic Modernism in the 1950s and 1960s.

Yet for all the startlingly original designs that befuddled critics in the Modern mainstream, some of Wright's most audacious designs—designs that matched even Bruce Goff's adventurous pursuit of innovation—were not built. A 1946 house jutting out of a cliff edge overlooking the Golden Gate for V. C. Morris supports a series of cantilevering, circular pods on a telescoping bracket-pier. One of the most daring designs was the Play Resort for Huntington Hartford (1947). Set in a dry, craggy landscape, the structure created its own enormous triangular crags of concrete growing out of the mountain as moorings for cantilevered pods. From circular pools embedded in the artificial slopes, water spills down the exposed side of the pool.[7] Its unflinching prominence and abstracted landscape forms echoed the Strong Automobile Objective (1925), but the jutting saucer-like pods capped with glass domes tip the design well into ultramodern territory. It is primarily sculptural composition, not disciplined by the rigorous geometric modules or grids Wright usually employed. This trajectory of design—landscape forms placed *on*, not *of* the hill, and reached via snaking roadways—continued in the Donahoe Triptych (1959), a house which bridged, clung to, and jutted out from the mountainside.

Other unbuilt designs demonstrated Wright's continuing interest in the circular geometry and domes he used in the Sol Friedman and David Wright houses, and in the Marin County Civic Center. For an enormous mansion, the Boulder House for Sr. Bailleres in Acapulco, Wright arched the living spaces with a shallow dome, leaving the periphery for views of the bay and mountains.[8] And for Crownfield, an unbuilt house for Robert Windfohr, Wright imagined a collection of domes with centers of glass tubing, as he had used at the Johnson Wax building.

Today all of these efforts deserve reconsideration as individual designs and as a group of work by a noteworthy architect. The sweeping angular rooflines of the Boomer, the Blair, the Elam, the Ablin houses (echoing the 1947 Unitarian Meeting House) create unmistakable exterior profiles and kinetic interior spaces. The triangular plans and wings of the Gillin and the McCartney houses gracefully unite indoor and outdoor spaces. The circular realms of the David Wright, the Sol Friedman, and the many hemicycle houses show a firm mastery of complex, intertwined shapes.

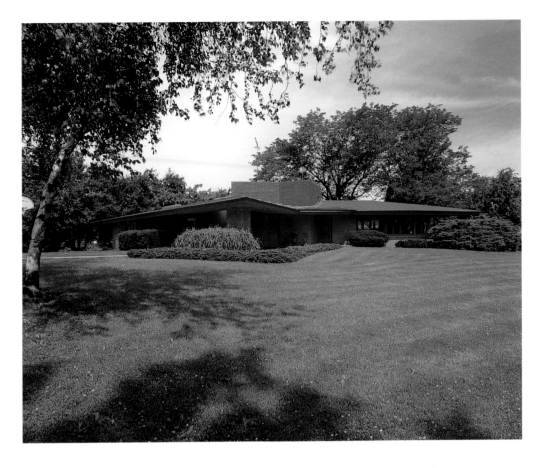

TRIANGULAR MODULE HOUSES
Above: Jack Lamberson House, Oskaloosa, Iowa, 1947

Opposite page, top, left to right: Carlton and Margaret Wall House (Snowflake), Plymouth, Michigan, 1941; Helen and Ward McCartney House, Parkwyn Village, Kalamazoo, Michigan, 1949

Opposite page, middle, left to right: Berenice and Richard Smith House, Jefferson, Wisconsin, 1950; Margaret and Patrick Kinney House, Lancaster, Wisconsin, 1951

Opposite page, bottom, left to right: Dorothy Ann and Sterling Kinney House, Amarillo, Texas, 1957 (1961); E. Clarke Arnold House, Columbus, Wisconsin, 1954

Lowell and Agnes Walter House

Wright was often true to his oft-stated principle that a house should grow from its site and structure. The Walter House (1945) draws much from its location on a rise next to a river in Iowa. The house's living room (Wright called it the garden room) is angled to views up and down the river; glass walls make the panorama an integral part of the experience of the house. The roof structure is concrete, and Wright resolves the edge of the roof in a manner both simple and expressive of that material: the roof extends out from the walls and then curves upward in one clean shape. Easy to form, this roof creates not a hard-edged fascia, but a soft edge. The design continues the concepts of Fallingwater; the public rooms are generous, squared-off, and lined with glass; the ceiling is prominent and lightened with trellises and skylights. The house is graceful, filled with light, and utterly unlike any conventional house. The clean lines of the upswept soffit instantly became a part of the Modern vocabulary of many other architects as an alternative to the hard-machined lines of International Style Modernism.

Like many other Wright houses of this optimistic era at war's end, this house was the house of the future, available today. In the Walter House, a manufactured Pullman bathroom unit added yet another touch of modern efficiency: this useful piece of technology included metal tub, sink, and toilet in one streamlined unit, a harbinger of the affordable factory-built houses which might be fabricated and trucked (or helicoptered) to a building site. As Wright houses were published in national magazines and local press, they became emblems of the future. If anything, they appeared even more modern than the flat-roofed cube-like forms of the International Style, which had taken the public's fancy in the 1930s. Organic architecture was offering a fresh and often warmer vision of tomorrow.

David and Gladys Wright House

A widely-published Wright design was an extraordinary architectural concoction: a house of swirling curves and circles, levitated above the ground, approached on sweeping ramps, built of concrete block, and untethered to any conventions of form and structure. The design began as a vivid, uncompromising conceptual prototype for "How to Live in the Southwest," and then was reworked and realized for Wright's son David, who worked for a concrete company in Phoenix. Like the spiraling Guggenheim famously under construction in New York in the same years, David Wright's house showed the public tangible proof of a new architecture.

In this design much more so than in the Sol Friedman House or his several hemicycle house designs, Wright broke open the circle and used its arcs in discrete but overlapping segments to create the indoor and outdoor spaces. As much as any Wright design of these years, it showed a more strikingly original idea about architecture than anything in the mainstream profession. Such formal audacity enraged many architects as ostentatious; many others were enthralled by its inventiveness. For all the complexities and ornateness of the concept, structure, and forms, it held together as a piece of architecture. The spaces were paramount: the curving living room was lifted above the surrounding citrus groves to enhance the view. The details meshed: curves and circles harmoniously governed the design in

everything from the arrangement of rooms to the design of the carpet. Though Wright had promoted his custom-designed textile block system since the 1920s, this house was constructed primarily of standard concrete block, with custom-designed ornamented blocks in strategic places. He was willing to use the off-the-shelf block to show the potential of a material others considered mundane, and he did this frequently through the 1950s.

Supremely photogenic, the strong curving walls of the house were set in a garden of pools and cars. It was a tour de force design. It trumpeted Wright's unconventionality and his claim to have an alternative for those people and architects not content with the glass boxes that dominated establishment Modernism.

Odd though the forms may have been, it was so adeptly conceived and executed that it could not be ignored.

John Gillin House

By the 1950s, the window wall was a staple of Modern architecture. Mating the newly evolved technologies of large plate-glass fabrication and aluminum or steel frames with a spatial concept of unifying indoors and outdoors, the glass wall was a distinguishing icon of Modern design—perhaps the single element that most distinguished it from all previous eras. The glass wall allowed architecture to perform its age-old purpose of sheltering inhabitants without trapping them in a dark box. Wright had no patent on the idea, which was used brilliantly in the 1950s by Richard Neutra, Mies van der Rohe, Craig Ellwood, Pierre Koenig, John Lautner, Philip Johnson, Marcel Breuer, and many other architects.

Wright used glass walls often, but in the Gillin House (1950) in Dallas he explored its impact on interior and openness to a greater extent than in any previous house. A long glass wall fronts most of the entire garden side of the house: it uses sliding glass doors, which are true window walls, not the typical French doors rooted in tradition. It angles to follow the house's sprawling wings. Where Philip Johnson used glass to create a solid geometric box, Wright used it to create an uninterrupted expanse between floor and ceiling. Elaborating on glass's inherent openness, he developed one of his most open floor plans. The long spacious area looking out on the garden and pool includes zones for the living room, dining room, and fireplace inglenook, laid out in a leisurely manner unlike the usually tightly woven geometries of a Wright house. He uses not walls but the soffits, coffers, and planes of the ceilings to define the individual spaces.

Topped by a copper roof and ornamental spire, the large Gillin residence demonstrates yet another way in which Wright's fertile imagination could embody a concept of space and structure in an original way. In its long, low apparently rambling profile, the house fitted in quite comfortably with the contemporary ranch houses of new suburban cities like Dallas or Phoenix. The Gillin House was decidedly non-urban, contradicting the architectural establishment's focus on traditional urban life. But in the way that its rich details related as an organic unity with the large-scale plan and structure of the house, the house was distinctively Wrightian.

Harold Price, Sr., House

The vacation house he designed for one of his most loyal patrons, Herbert Price, took Wright in yet another direction—one that has no other built example. The desert climate inspired an outdoor living room at the center of the long narrow house. The high ceiling is held aloft on tall tapering columns—columns that taper from a narrow base to a wide-shouldered top. Standard concrete blocks form the walls.

While the house is clearly Wrightian, it is a unique design. The idea of an outdoor living room is a natural result from his long insistence that architectural form should respond to the climate and site, but the Price House (1954) is long and linear with no angular or circular flourishes. Its two wings—one for guests, one for owner—are only slightly angled to the terrain. The starkness of the broad concrete block walls is moderated by architectural ornament, but

HEMICYCLE HOUSES

Top row, left to right: Kenneth and Phyllis Laurent House, Rockford, Illinois, 1949; Dudley Spencer House, Wilmington, Delaware, 1956

Bottom row, left to right: Clifton and George Lewis House (Spring House), Tallahassee, Florida, 1952; Louis Marden House, McLean, Virginia, 1953; Robert D. Winn House, Kalamazoo, Michigan, 1950, (Parkwyn Village)

Opposite page: Lillian and Curtis Meyer House, Galesburg, Michigan, 1948, (Galesburg Country Homes)

the house has an austere character that is unusual for Wright.

Harriet and Randall Fawcett House

In contrast to the Price House in Phoenix, the Fawcett House (1955) in rural Los Banos, California, is a more luxurious design. It is also constructed of concrete block, but because the plan is based on a triangular rather than square module those block walls become more lively. The oblique angles of the house embrace an open-air patio that unites the separate, covered wings of the house. Each row of blocks in the concrete block walls are stepped in, creating battered walls throughout the house. Outside they vividly project the unconventional character of the architecture; inside they create bowls, inglenooks, and open space for built-in couches with which Wright re-invents the traditional spaces of a house. The extremities of the building and the main entry end in angular wall elements and upswept rooflines that emphatically link the house to the broad Central Valley sky. Shallow decorative urns—which Wright used throughout his entire career—sit on top of these irregular forms to punctuate the view. Average in size, the house is not an estate like Auldbrass or Wingspread, and yet the design is as striking and original as other moderate-sized houses by Wright, such as the Walter House (1945), the Walker House (1948), or the David Wright House (1950). He could be startlingly creative on any scale of architecture.

* * *

At the age of eighty-three in 1950, Wright was a different character than the arty but bourgeois family man of fifty years earlier. He now carried himself as a lion and a prophet. He had carefully developed this persona as a means of catching people's attention and obtaining commissions—and his ego gloried in the attention he drew. Wright and his wife Olgivanna had created a community of the arts around themselves, and this community served as a source of workers and a sounding board for their ideas. The Taliesin community was often tempestuous; at times one wonders how Wright accomplished any work at all with the whirl of music and dance concerts, the building of new barns and roads, and the conflict of personalities among many artistic souls.

Under Olgivanna's eye and instigation, life at Taliesin churned and stewed. Trained by Georgi Gurdjieff in her native Europe, the Montenegran Olgivanna lived by a philosophy of strength produced through struggle—even if the struggle was artificially induced. Add to that Wright's own outsized ego, his hasty assumption of disloyalty at the smallest slights by his apprentices, and the soap opera manipulation of friendships, marriages, and personalities, and one can imagine the challenging environment of Taliesin. Still, the respect for beauty brought to simple flower arrangements and food preparation, the weekly musicales, the leisurely picnics in the fields of Spring Green,

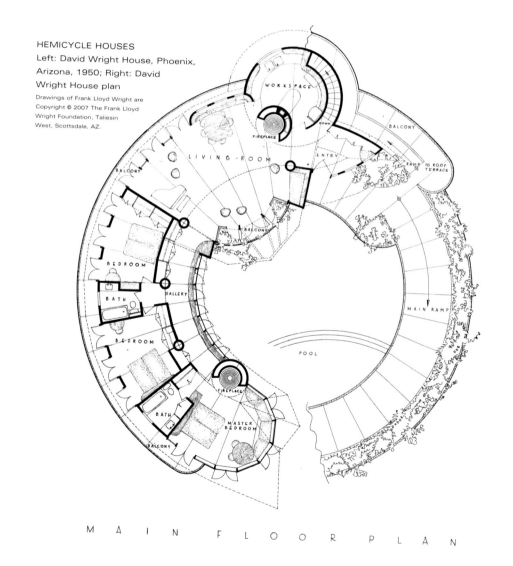

HEMICYCLE HOUSES
Left: David Wright House, Phoenix, Arizona, 1950; Right: David Wright House plan

Drawings of Frank Lloyd Wright are Copyright © 2007 The Frank Lloyd Wright Foundation, Taliesin West, Scottsdale, AZ.

WORKSPACE

FIREPLACE

BALCONY

LIVING ROOM

BALCONY

ENTRY

RAMP TO ROOF TERRACE

BEDROOM

BALCONY

GALLERY

BATH

MAIN RAMP

BEDROOM

POOL

FIREPLACE

BATH

MASTER BEDROOM

BALCONY

M A I N   F L O O R   P L A N

CIRCULAR PLAN
Top: Sol Friedman House, Pleasantville, New York, 1947, Usonia Homes; Middle: Julia and Duey Wright House, Wausau, Wisconsin, 1956; Bottom: Aime and Norman Lykes House, Phoenix, Arizona, 1959

Wisconsin, the hijinks of lively and creative young people, and the chance to hear about architecture directly from the mouth of one of the greatest architects of the century made Taliesin worth the struggle for many.

Taliesin served many of Wright's needs well. Around him constantly was a pool of young men (and some women) who would do his bidding and stoke his ego, calling him only "Mr. Wright" to his face (and "Daddy Frank" behind his back). He seemed to draw on the atmosphere of youthful vitality, and he remained physically and intellectually vigorous until his death. Wright's fame brought him many witty, knowledgeable, and famous friends who visited Taliesin for picnics, concerts, and performances: Clare Booth Luce, Alexander Woollcott, Paul Robeson, Adlai Stevenson, Charles Laughton, and Carl Sandburg. During Wright's life, the camp in out-of-the-way Scottsdale was far from isolated, and his buoyant egotism was quite bearable. After his death, however, the community's insularity grew. Its sense of itself as a lone citadel of true culture was hard pressed to sustain Taliesin after he died.

The lives of many artists are untidy and dysfunctional, and Wright's was no different. Though in 1950 his was one of the larger architecture firms in the nation, Wright's office was far from the model of organizational clarity that launched other major firms such as Welton Becket and Associates (now Ellerbe Becket) and Skidmore, Owings & Merrill into the steady and established offices they are today. Wright could be reckless and aggressive in getting clients—and in losing them. He insisted that the only phone at Taliesin West should be in his office; his apprentices had to drive into town and use a pay phone to call clients and job supervisors, spreading drawings out on the hood of their car.[9]

Taliesin could be a difficult place. But it was, after all, the atmosphere in which the Guggenheim Museum, the Price Tower, and the Usonian houses were conceived and brought to reality.

NATURE

A central message repeated in Wright's press in the 1950s (whether in *House Beautiful*, *Life*, local newspapers, or Wright's own writings) is the absolute necessity for architecture to relate to nature. In an increasingly suburbanized America, the yearning for a view of nature from your picture window was strong, and Wright responded. Fallingwater is perhaps the ultimate visual and spatial statement of this principle, but other Wright houses reinforced it. The Walter House (1945) looks out over a peaceful river view in the Midwest. The Hagan House (1954) faces a forest, and the Bott House (1957) a river valley at the confluence of the Kansas and Missouri rivers and the towers of downtown Kansas City. The house for Mrs. Clinton Walker in Carmel was one of Wright's most dramatic opportunities: built on a rocky promontory jutting into the Pacific Ocean on Carmel Bay, the house was a profound image of human ingenuity confidently mingling with the powerful surging forces of nature.

Rising from the rocky crag, most of the house is built of the richly golden native stone, but the prow of the house, thrust out toward the pounding waves, is an hexagonal glass observatory. It provides warm shelter from the elements for the resident even as it offers an unparalleled close-up panorama of nature's wild beauty. The window wall circumscribing the living room steps outward, counter-intuitively. The glass's thin steel frame—the barest of structures that modern technology allowed—fades away so as not to interfere with the feeling of oneness with nature. The stepped configuration also solved the problem of steady sea breezes blowing directly into the house; while the vertical panes are fixed in place, the horizontal panes are operable vents that let fresh air into the glass observatory.

GEOMETRY

In his later years Wright's expressive searches focused on the potential of various geometries in shaping his house designs. Everything in these designs grew, organically, from a selected basic module a few square feet in area. Whether a square, circle, triangle, or parallelogram, this module determined almost every other aspects of the design: the shape of rooms, the placement of walls, kitchens and bathrooms, the relation of one wing to another, and the house's footprint on the site.

Of course geometry had always been in Wright's fingertips, ostensibly since his mother introduced the child Wright to the tactile shapes of the Froebel blocks. In his early years the Prairie houses and the Los Angeles textile-block houses had been based on large, often complex geometric patterns of long central and secondary axes, punctuated by large square or rectangular spaces. Now in the mid-century he began looking deeper into an underlying indivisible unit, a conceptual building block, which could be multiplied and arranged to create larger spaces. The first breakthrough design was the Hanna House (1936); its hexagonal module created a startling house with no right angles. All walls, all rooms opened up in the open embrace of the hexagon's oblique angles, expressed both vertically and horizontally. Instead of long flat walls, these walls were indeterminate and gently shaped a flowing interior space. He repeated this module in the smaller Bazett House (1939) nearby, but then moved on; his houses after these hexagonal experiments show how

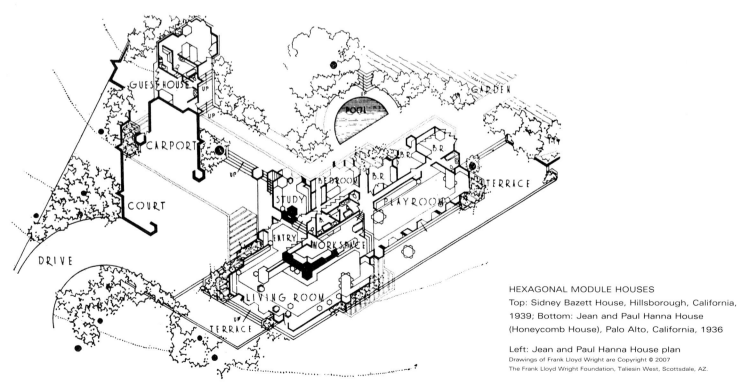

HEXAGONAL MODULE HOUSES
Top: Sidney Bazett House, Hillsborough, California, 1939; Bottom: Jean and Paul Hanna House (Honeycomb House), Palo Alto, California, 1936

Left: Jean and Paul Hanna House plan
Drawings of Frank Lloyd Wright are Copyright © 2007
The Frank Lloyd Wright Foundation, Taliesin West, Scottsdale, AZ.

Wright's inquiring mind was not satisfied with repeating a formula; he had to improve it. And so the hexagon evolved into systems of triangle and parallelogram modules, which proved more satisfying to design. Oblique angles were still implicit in these modules, allowing for the easy-going placement of walls and flowing space without the abruptness of right angles; but the directionality of the triangles' sides also helped lay out entire wings of a house in a more unifying manner.

Though Wright as a self-styled prophet proclaimed sweeping aesthetic generalizations ("Never paint natural wood"; "A house should be of the hill, never on it"), Wright as an artist never hesitated to break his own rules. His inspiration in the moment took him to other places. Even with his definitive geometric modules, Wright would explore inventive aberrations, as seen in the Armstrong and Greenberg houses. The latter, atypically, jams three grids together in a jarring collision, rather than a smooth transition.

Still other mid-century Wright designs stand at a point between the irregularity of natural forms and the orderly abstraction of geometry. As early as the 1920s, he played with tilting walls that tweaked gravity in a series of house barges and cabins (never built) for Lake Tahoe. The unbuilt house for Mrs. Samuel William Gladney (1926) in Ft. Worth, Texas demonstrated the same interest in folded planes and spire extensions that caused the ends of the house to taper off into the ether.[10] Once he had seen the stark escarpments of the Arizona desert, stripped of vegetation, his houses often grew from sloping terraced walls that echoed natural shapes, as in the Rose Pauson House (1939). The Neils House (1949) takes these angled, irregular forms up into the walls of the house itself, creating crystalline forms rendered in concrete, stone, and wood.

Wright was also fearless about curves. Most modernists shied from them except as carefully controlled accents; Wright—like that other apostate, Oscar Niemeyer—dived into them. Wright preferred perfect circles or arcs. These tantalizing shapes played a rhetorical role, too: they broke the hegemony of the right-angled box (the architectural

convention from the beginning of time) as a symbol of a new age of architecture. The proposed Ralph Jester House (1938) established his ideas about how to build with circles. Designed for Southern California's benign climate, Wright designed several circular structures around an open-air garden. The unbuilt Burlingham House (1941) for El Paso, Texas, furthered these explorations.[11] When he actually built a house of circles, however, it was in the less-welcoming climate of New York. The Sol Friedman House (1948) used the circle as the enclosing boundary, with the interior space divided into segments. A variation on the perfect circle was the hemicycle, a curving segment of a circle, which Wright used in a half-dozen houses beginning with the second Jacobs House in 1944. The curving houses turned large concave glass walls toward the path of the sun, allowing sunlight to warm concrete floors and brick or stone walls in these passive solar designs—another aspect of Organic designing with nature. The plans of the hemicycles were quite similar (bedroom wings at one side, a large open living space, and a central brick block for kitchen anchoring the house), though several (see the 1955 Rayward House) were expanded with additions that showed how Wright could smoothly add to an unusual plan geometry.

* * *

Residences constituted the majority of Wright's buildings in the last two decades of his life, but were not the primary focus for his attention. A series of large public and private commissions came his way and often dominated his interest; he left much of the actual work of designing and constructing the Usonian house commissions to John Howe, an able and longtime Taliesin Fellow. Wright himself focused on the string of larger public commissions: the Johnson Wax

headquarters, Florida Southern College, the Kansas City Community Church (1940), the Guggenheim Museum (commissioned in 1943, completed in 1959), the Unitarian Meeting House (1947), the V. C. Morris Shop (1948), the Price Tower (1948), the Beth Shalom Synagogue (1948), the Humphrey Theater (1948), the Greek Orthodox Church (1956), the Marin County Civic Center (1959), as well as numerous projects not built. These large projects sometimes reflected the themes also explored in the houses: the curve as a spatial and structural form, the use of geometric ornament, and the use of modern materials such as aluminum and plastic.

Wright's influence on the mid-century was enormous. He courted this attention, of course; it was his primary means of attracting

new clients. Most architects, whether loving or hating him, had to deal with his presence and ideas. Many took up his ideas as their own. Through large firms such as MacKie and Kamrath and Anshen and Allen, Organic concepts spread to highrises and institutional buildings. Through the ranch house, Wright's championing of the suburban home, open to nature for the modern family, spread to the mass public. Through hundreds of ultramodern restaurants built along the boulevards and commercial strips of the postwar suburban cities for the car-mobile public, his ideas of free-flowing spaces, structurally expressive rooflines, and gardens brought indoors could be enjoyed by the average person. Though critics labeled these "Googie" and ersatz Organic, they testified to the success of his concepts. Through

ULTRAMODERN
Top row, left to right: Charles Glore House, Lake Forest, Illinois, 1951; Lewis Goddard House, Plymouth, Michigan, 1953; Karen Johnson (Keland) House, Racine, Wisconsin, 1954;

Bottom row, left to right: Robert Sunday House, Marshalltown, Iowa, 1955 (1963); Carl Schultz House, Saint Joseph, Michigan, 1957 (1959); Frank and Eloise Bott House, Kansas City, Missouri, 1957 (1963)

Opposite page, top: I. N. Hagan House, Chalkhill, Pennsylvania, 1954; Bottom: Conrad Edward and Evelyn Gordon House, Wilsonville, Oregon, 1956 (1964)

Previous pages 32–33, left: Richard and Madelyn Davis House, Marion, Indiana, 1950; Right: Douglas and Jackie Grant House, Cedar Rapids, Iowa, 1946

House Beautiful, Life, and other popular magazines, editors regularly boosted his ideas and buildings.

While his vision frequently proved him an accurate prophet, this was not always the case. His insistence on a horizontal board and batten wall (and other structural innovations) for his average-person's Usonian house proved unworkable in the world of tract housing; the bland but easily fabricated wood stud wall sheathed in wall board proved more flexible for the needs of mass-produced housing than Wright's more exotic inventions. The growing corporativism of society and architecture also isolated Wright and his deep-rooted faith in the individual. His unwillingness to grapple with such practical constraining factors in the new society pushed him out into the cold.

Wright's philosophy of "Beauty" also set him at odds with mid-century trends. He spoke of beauty as a romantic, Emersonian spiritual quality; but architecture in the second half of the twentieth century, swayed by Modern art, detached beauty from its traditional high culture roots and often embraced a gritty, utilitarian, vernacular, and at times shocking sense of beauty. Exposed steel columns and galvanized heating ducts, rusting Cor-ten steel, austere geometric forms, and ragged concrete were the new stuff of beauty. Wright's abiding sense of the House Beautiful (a name used for the magazine which he helped to found in the 1890s) was something quite different.

Wright's houses in the last twenty years of his life push far beyond the Prairie houses. Several are acknowledged masterpieces of world architecture: Fallingwater, the Walker House, the Jacobs House II. But others make critics uneasy to this day; the extreme unconventionality of a design like the Huntington Hartford Play Resort, though never built, raises pointed questions: was Wright on a solitary path of aesthetic exploration that took him so far beyond accepted taste that society never caught up with him? Or was he prodded by his ego, his public persona, and perhaps his waning skills to delve into extremes of form to sustain the world's attention? Or was the profession's frequent neglect of the booming suburbs as serious architecture (where Wright built most of his houses in this period) to blame for the neglect of the ideas Wright wanted to raise?

And so we are left with the odd situation of Frank Lloyd Wright being America's most famous architect almost a half century after his death, and yet one whose entire work is still not entirely known or appreciated. His Prairie designs have achieved an unassailable status, both professionally and popularly; the Guggenheim Museum and Johnson Wax headquarters are considered bedrock icons that cement Wright's reputation when most other architects of the time are relegated to history books. But what about the rest of his later work?

Each house, each structure was a piece of Wright's master plan to transform the United States into Broadacre City. While he was cynical about the "mob-ocracy" he saw around him, Wright was essentially optimistic. The future, with the ever-changing potential of technology and the enduring serenity of nature, promised lives of infinite variety. He did his best to design homes that would reflect these possibilities and encourage that search.●

ULTRAMODERN
Above: Price Tower, Bartlesville, Oklahoma, 1952 (1953–1956)

Opposite page: Quintin and Ruth Blair House, Cody, Wyoming, 1952

Left to right: Pfeiffer Chapel, Florida
Southern College, Lakeland, Florida, 1938;
Anderton Court Shops, Beverly Hills,
California, 1952; Beth Sholom Synagogue,
Elkins Park, Pennsylvania, 1954

Frank Lloyd Wright and World War II, 1939–45

By John Zukowsky

World War II brought out the best and worst in people. It was a time when neutral countries and their citizens, such as those in the United States, were torn between isolationist tendencies and support of the belligerents. Architects and architectural aficionados were no exception. The support of German military advances in Poland and France during 1939–40, as given by Philip Johnson in the anti-Semitic newspaper *Social Justice*, is one of the oft-cited instances of an architect taking sides in this early stage of the war before America's entry into the fray in December 1941. Modernists of German descent such as Paul Schweikher saw Germany's early successes on the battlefield as a redressing of the humiliations brought on that nation after the stiff terms imposed by the Treaty of Versailles at the close of World War I.[1] In some ways Frank Lloyd Wright also supported those early German victories, at least inadvertently.

In his publication *A Taliesin Square-Paper: A Nonpolitical Voice from our Democratic Minority* (May 15, 1941) he wrote about Germany's impending defeat of the British Empire despite the greatness of Britain's Royal Navy, and further that ". . . aid to England is impossible except to prolong the death agony of a great empire." He also wrote "I love England but I hate Empire . . . ." Throughout he attacks President Franklin Delano Roosevelt and his supporters as ". . . hangovers from early days still trying to keep our eastern states loyal English colonies." Yet, upon request from the *News Chronicle of London*, Wright wrote an article expressing his ideas for building London

after the German blitz in a decentralized way, in keeping with his ideas for Broadacre City. In many ways this was a repeat performance of a not surprisingly controversial speech he gave to the Royal Institute of British Architects in 1939, just months before war began in Europe. Although he might not have liked the following comparison, his support of decentralized architectural resources is not that dissimilar, in overall principle, to what European modernists such as Ludwig Hilberseimer proposed in his books such as *The New City* (1944) and the *New Regional Pattern* (1949). The difference, however, lies in Wright's buildings compared with those of European modernists, whom he asserted misunderstood him and his efforts to create an indigenous American architecture through democratic Usonian building. In a September 14, 1940 telegram to the Museum of Modern Art about his forthcoming exhibition, Wright said he was ". . . tired of the conspiracy of this foreign clique."[2] Later, in *A Taliesin Square-Paper* (August 24, 1941) he issued his own "Declaration of Independence" in an article entitled "Usonia, Usonia South, and New England." In it he continually derides President Roosevelt's tendencies to get America involved in the war to support Britain, and he even goes so far as to create his ideal tri-state federation called the United States of North America, which includes Usonia, Usonia South, and New England. His claim for increased efficiency of three versus forty-eight states is both ironic and contradictory, considering his advocacy for decentralized over centralized environments. But his map's message is obvious: to

separate the architecturally and politically contaminated "New England"—a section of the nation from Washington, D.C., Maryland, and Pennsylvania, north up through Maine, all of which he felt was tied to the cultural baggage of Europe and Britain—from the truly American remainder of the nation, which would be free of the "foreign influence" of what he, at one time earlier, termed "Old Europe." Although we have seen the resurrection of this appellation used in recent years, this anti-Europeanism and specifically anti-British feeling might seem justifiably shocking to many, but placed within the context of the time prior to America's entry into the war, it is less so. Other more prominent Americans shared similar sentiments towards Britain and President Roosevelt and initially supported American isolationism. They range from aviation record setter Charles Lindbergh to World War I hero and industrialist Eddie Rickenbacker.[3] But any questions about American support for entering the war changed on December 7, 1941, with the Japanese attack on Pearl Harbor—except, perhaps, in Wright's world.

During 1941–45 while America was one of the Allies fighting the Axis Powers, the vocal and visible Wright became a bit more of a background figure, but he still decried any support of the war effort. Many American architects, particularly younger ones, served in the military including the Army Corps of Engineers and Navy's Construction Battalion (CB) or 'Seabees.' For instance, Myron Goldsmith who engineered a number of postwar skyscrapers for Skidmore, Owings

& Merrill learned about construction firsthand in the Corps of Engineers. Bruce Goff, a prewar follower of Wright, paved his way to a postwar career producing "organic" architecture after serving as a Seabee and creating individualist designs incorporating found materials, much as he did after the war. Older architects such as Erich Mendelsohn and Konrad Wachsmann actively participated with American industry and the U.S. military to create German and Japanese constructions that were used to test the efficiency of high explosive and incendiary bombs. Others such as Bertrand Goldberg volunteered to create material-saving designs for the Board of Economic Warfare and the Office of Strategic Services (O.S.S.), such as shipping crates for weapons that could be recycled into housing for troops. Authors have stated that Wright had very few commissions in this time period except for small private jobs and the possibility of consulting on a film version of the novel *The Fountainhead*. His previous statements against Britain and Roosevelt, his official encouragement of apprentices to oppose conscription as Conscientious Objectors, and his alienation of a variety of prominent cultural personalities with anti-war statements, most certainly influenced Wright's inability to secure government commissions[4]—unlike architectural consortia and larger partnerships such as Skidmore, Owings & Merrill, whose government connections before the war led them to large-scale jobs during and after the war. Wright was at least fortunate to have continuing work for corporate clients such as S.C. Johnson & Son in Racine, Wisconsin (the Johnson Research Tower and Lab, 1944), and institutional buildings added to his campus at Florida Southern College, even though some were not completed until the end of the war.

Wright also had a few private clients who had him completing houses designed at

the beginning of the war and, in one notable case, designing a home in 1944—his second house for Herbert and Katherine Jacobs in Middletown, Wisconsin, seen above, (the first being the earliest Usonian example from 1936). This important wartime commission was the first solar hemicycle house that Wright designed, and its semi-circular form of locally quarried stone, built into a berm within the landscape, set the tone for a number of his postwar homes, which were often decidedly different than the rectilinear prewar Usonian homes. Perhaps the European-like clean lines and skeletal structure of prewar Usonians may have been something that Wright wanted to leave behind for a more indigenous American architecture.

It is true that Wright occasionally used curved and circular forms in the mid- to late-1930s, including the Johnson Wax Building of 1936 and especially the unexecuted Ralph Jester House of 1938 for Palos Verdes, California, but they did not permeate his work until the post-World War II period, particularly in the proposed Kaufmann House for Palm Springs in 1951, the Winn House in Kalamazoo from 1950, the proposed Huntington Hartford House and Sports Club in Hollywood, both 1947, and the renowned Guggenheim Museum, first designed 1943–44 but constructed 1956. The so-called second Jacobs House of 1944–48 serves as a tangible expression of Wright's attitudes toward an indigenous form integrated into the American landscape in what he would have called, during the 1940s, the state of Usonia. One might be tempted to speculate that this was his bunker, a retreat from the war's environment into the landscape, but

that would mean that he would have had to acknowledge some shame for his earlier wartime statements. Considering the long history of his own sense of architectural importance, and his almost comical attempts at getting wartime government contracts, even from the super-secret O.S.S., I doubt that any deeper psychological motives underlie this low-key berm design that did visibly relate to his idea of a democratic American architecture that grows out of Usonia's landscape.

The end of World War II and the 1950s economic boom brought Wright increased work, particularly residential jobs, and continued public recognition to the point of becoming a television celebrity interviewed by Hugh Downs in 1953 and Mike Wallace in 1957. But Wright's proposals—such as his Mile High Skyscraper for Chicago in 1956—came to nothing as Skidmore, Owings & Merrill got the big Air Force Academy commission in 1954 and, within a few years of Wright's 1959 death, built the 100-story John Hancock Tower in Chicago (1965–69). As with his earlier works in relation to his career, Wright's wartime words and deeds led him to what happened in that postwar era, for better or worse. •

Top, above, and right: Herbert and Katherine Jacobs House II, Middleton, Wisconsin, 1944

Exuberant Fifties: Wright and the Guggenheim

By Monica Ramírez Montagut

If Frank Lloyd Wright's life embodies the cyclical hopes and disillusionments of the industrial age, the history of Wright's Solomon R. Guggenheim Museum (1943–1959) embodies the pre- and postwar sentiment of the fifties and a turn of modern architecture to more organic and plastic forms. The war's demand for materials caused a major delay in the museum's construction and contributed in part to the lengthy sixteen year history[1] and the raising spiral museum consolidated what was an emerging tendency amongst the "second generation" of Modern architects, an exuberant Modernism at the time of the so-called crisis of Modern architecture.[2]

By the early 1950s Modern architecture was commonly identified with sleek and rationally composed simple geometric volumes, cleansed of superficial ornament and built with technological innovations. And thus Modern architecture came to be mainly identified as cold and rational, objective and machinelike, with social concerns generally associated to an urban scale. This understanding of architecture was best represented by Le Corbusier and not generally linked to Wright, for Wright's architecture was considered warm, expressionistic, emotional, highly personal, hand crafted and primarily suburban. Yet in spite of Wright's rather marginal position to modern architecture,[3] the Guggenheim Museum came to be considered his masterwork of the fifties and an icon of Mid-Century Modern.

More than eighty years old by 1950, Wright's life was tightly linked to the intense developments of the museum. The decade had started in a less than positive tone as Solomon Guggenheim had died recently[4] and the audacity of the design was gaining many adversaries such as the Fifth Avenue Association. Yet, 1952 appeared to be prolific. Plan submissions for the museum were well underway and a retrospective exhibition on Wright's work, *60 Years of Living Architecture,* was touring countries such as Italy and Mexico and intended to be housed in the temporary pavilion designed by him at the museum's grounds in 1953. Optimism also filled the air as the Oil Pipeline headquarters for the Price Company was under construction in Oklahoma, materializing Wright's long awaited ideas for plasticity in the structure of a skyscraper.[5] Wright envisioned a monolithic structure where each surface—wall, ceiling, and floor—seamlessly engaged each other to create continuity and an integral whole. Seeing that postwar America was bringing unfinished projects to completion, Wright developed some of his most inspired projects such as the Mile High skyscraper, the Greek Orthodox Church in Wisconsin, The Golden Beacon Tower, and more than twenty private residences.

These high spirits were constantly tested, however, by struggles between Wright and the designated director of the museum since 1952, James Johnson Sweeney. Sweeney and a roster of renowned artists[6] expected the museum to have "traditional" Modern spaces: to be orthogonal, white, and artificially illuminated. Wright, on the other hand, refused to present paintings in the "incongruous room of the old static architecture"[7] and wanted to create an "uninterrupted unit" between the building and the artwork. Just as he had accomplished for the structure of the Price Tower, Wright wanted the Guggenheim to achieve "a harmonious fluidity" between the spiral floor plan and its slanted walls, the multilevel ramp and its seamless parapets, and he did.

Wright's last disagreement with Sweeney[8] regarded the color of the interior of the museum. The director requested stark white and Wright opposed explaining that white was the loudest color of all and proposed ivory.[9] Every detail was important for Wright in a museum he had come to denominate an "Archeseum" for it represented a closing statement for his own views on architecture. The disagreements between Sweeney and Wright symbolized a much larger struggle taking place in the architectural world.

The second generation of Modern architects—such as Charles Eames and Eero Saarinen, for example—confronted similar established notions of Modern architecture. They questioned some of the precepts of early Modern architecture, considering them puritan, austere, and highly abstract. Their time demanded a more expressionistic

Frank Lloyd Wright, Hilla Rebay, and Solomon Guggenheim at the unveiling of the model for the Guggenheim, 1945. Photo by Ben Greenhaus. © 2007 Donald Greenhaus / Artists Rights Society (ARS), New York.

Left: Interior of The
Solomon R. Guggenheim
Museum, New York.
Photograph by William H.
Short © The Solomon R.
Guggenheim Foundation,
New York.

Opposite: Frank Lloyd
Wright at the Solomon
R. Guggenheim Museum
construction site, 1959.
Photograph by David
Heald © The Solomon R.
Guggenheim Foundation,
New York.

language that was colored with a certain postwar optimism. While complying with early Modern architecture's spirit of experimentation and technological, constructive, and material innovation, the younger architects parted from the rationally composed simple geometric volumes and engaged in search for more luxurious contours and injected their work with sensuousness and exuberant forms. They also explored color and even engaged certain historicisms. Like Wright, Eames and Saarinen not only challenged some of the established notions, they were also highly influenced by them.

As a young architecture student Charles Eames "was intrigued by Wright and considered his work to be an essential part of any architectural curriculum, but when he persisted in proposing Wright as a subject of study to his professors he ran into a wall of stubborn resistance."[10] He left to travel the world and, later on, opened his own firm. In 1935, intrigued by Eames' St. Mary's Church in Helena, Eliel Saarinen, the director of the Cranbrook Academy of Art in Michigan, contacted him. Eames was later invited to teach at Cranbrook and also met Eliel's son, Eero, establishing a life-long friendship. They worked together in the furniture designs for the 1940 MoMA competition "Organic Design in Home furnishings," which also suffered delays due to wartime restrictions affecting the availability of materials. In later design experimentations, Eames substituted metal for a warmer material: plywood. He pressed the plywood at different points and achieved a series of furniture characteristic for its complex curves. By the 1950s the technology developed by the war made available new plastics and previous plywood curves were then transferred to polyester plastic and fiberglass furniture. These new chairs achieved the Wrightian ideal of "plasticity," where all surfaces—arms, seat,

and back rests—were one continuous whole. Eventually the furniture was to be mass-produced and available to a broader audience.

A personal friend of his father Eliel, Eero Saarinen was also familiar not only with Wright's work but with Wright himself.[11] Saarinen acknowledged Wright's leadership in Modern architecture: "Tools alone do not make architecture. There must also be leadership to show the direction and thus the new architecture and its three great men —Frank Lloyd Wright, Le Corbusier, and Mies van der Rohe." Saarinen, however, ultimately dismissed him the same way Wright had dismissed his father: "Frank Lloyd Wright's influence comes from another era; his forms do also."[12] It was perhaps Saarinen's wife, Aline B. Saarinen, who was more objective in recognizing Wright's influence at the time and that of the Guggenheim in particular. In an article she wrote for the *New York Times* that described a tour she took, accompanied by Wright, during construction; she explained that young audiences were visiting the museum even in its unfinished state and were attracted, not only by the architect, but by its astonishing structure.[13]

Sculptural and spectacular shapes like that of the Eames' *La Chaise* and plastic chairs, Saarien's Kresge Auditorium and Trans World Airline Terminal, and Wright's Solomon R. Guggenheim Museum were garnering extraordinary popularity while simultaneously being highly criticized. Charles Eames was dismissed from Washington University because he was too modern; Eero Saarinen was described as a mannerist that was contributing to the decline of modern architecture and distancing from the premise "form follows function,"[14] and the Guggenheim was described as "one of Frank Lloyd Wright's most joyous monstrosities [...] A building that should be put in a museum to show how mad the twentieth century was."[15]

Now, madness is also a state of intense excitement or enthusiasm, and as such, these expressionistic forms were also being praised for providing a visual and sensual experience that filled the eye and the mind. They achieved a marriage between structure and space, becoming a fluid unity; and their expressivity initially criticized for being too literal was reconsidered as a positive element for communicating with a larger audience. The wide range of forms available also represented the demands of a diverse society with a broader appeal.

Today, as yet another generation of architects and designers grapples optimistically with the march of technology and all that it affords—from new materials to extraordinarily sophisticated computer software programs allowing for an abundance of exuberant and astonishing forms—the question of Wright and the fifties, and our perception of architectural innovation generally, remains an enduring one of timeless importance and vitality. •

Mid-Century
Modern Houses

Liliane and Edgar J. Kaufmann House

Fallingwater, Mill Run, Pennsylvania 1935

Fallingwater launched the fourth and most prolific chapter of Wright's career in the middle of the century. At the time the world generally considered Wright a figure from the past, so its astonishment at this design was palpable. Not only had he produced a building of self-evident imaginative originality rivaling anything else on the architectural scene, he had executed it with utter mastery and sensitivity.

Right: The approach from the forest to the front door beneath the squared archway. Opposite: Instead of placing the house to look out at the natural waterfall (a passive solution), Wright boldly sited the house astride the waterfall itself, as part of it.

Left: Concrete cantilevers jut out over the stream. Wright contrasts the vertical lines of natural stone piers with the horizontal lines of concrete, including the low balcony railings. Above: A suspended stairway cascades from the living room down to the water's surface as seen at left. Steel-framed glass encloses the stair in winter and slides back in summer.

Five views of the living room demonstrate Wright's masterful interweaving of rock structure, glass planes for light and views, and an exquisite layer of varied ornamental texture derived from stone, wood trim, and fabrics.

In his earliest home designs, Wright kitchens were strictly utilitarian,
as the province of servants. At Fallingwater the kitchen has become as highly designed
—and as architecturally integrated—as any other room in the house.

Above: Wright uses a standard bathroom sink of the period as a practical, functionally designed item seen against the natural stone walls. Right: Closet cabinet stops short of the ceiling, allowing a place for indirect artificial light to reflect against the white ceiling. Next page: The house is unmistakably an artifact of human culture, and yet it draws from the powerful natural setting of rock, forest, and stream.

Herbert and Katherine Jacobs House I

Madison, Wisconsin 1936 (1937)

Wright's fertile imagination could not be suppressed. Though he could design astonishing large houses like Fallingwater, he also designed small houses that could be built by the average middle class family, even during the Great Depression. This was the first Usonian house to be built. Its interplay of brick piers and horizontal wood planes is as sophisticated as Fallingwater, though at the same time a simple family home for an ordinary suburban site.

Right, top: The bank of windows at left frames the view from the living room; Right bottom: The angled wing holds the living room and kitchen. Far right: In contrast, the street face has only high clerestory windows to let in light.

Above left: The living room includes built-in bookshelves, seating, tables, and a writing nook.
Above right: Hall from bedrooms looking toward dining and living rooms. Opposite: The sturdy brick fireplace
anchors the house's open plan. Front door is to its left, kitchen and dining area are behind it.

Herbert Johnson House

Wingspread, Wind Point, Wisconsin 1937

Wingspread, another lavish estate, offered Wright the opportunity to show even more of his formal and spatial inventiveness.

Right, top: The master bedroom suite soars out from its brick pier in a joyful moment of architectural play. Right, bottom: Four wings spin outward across the flat site. Far right: A futuristic octagonal dome, pierced with windows, caps the great central hall of Wingspread; an observatory tops it.

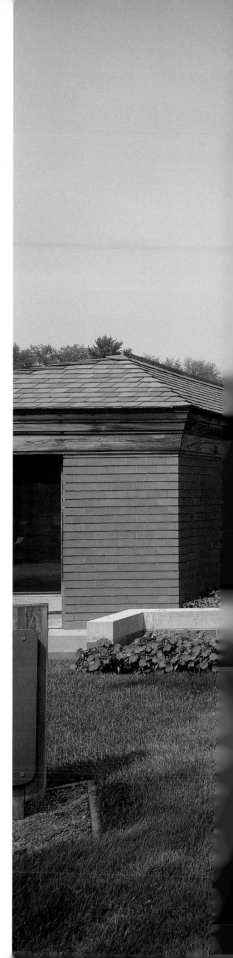

Left: The central hall. Above: The dome's windows let light down into the space,
while the spiral stair leads up to the widow's walk observatory.

Multiple levels of the central hall include living areas, musical rooms, dining area, and inglenooks. Warm red brick and natural wood provide the textures, colors, and ornament for the architecture—in sharp contrast to the painted plaster and egg-and-dart trim of traditional homes of the time. Next page: Since his Prairie houses thirty years before, Wright's aesthetic included horizontal lines and asymmetrical compositions. In his Mid-Century Modern designs he carries those themes even further.

Taliesin West

Scottsdale, Arizona 1938

Fresh ideas poured from Wright's fertile creativity. Another great house, Taliesin West, built for Wright himself, was as expertly developed and executed as Fallingwater and Wingspread. It would serve as laboratory for many spatial and formal ideas Wright would explore over the next twenty years.

Far right: The sloping roof of the drafting room at left contrasts with the living quarters at right. Above, right: Entry court to compound and drafting room. Below, right: A new formal vocabulary of slanted concrete walls embedded with desert rock (and contrasting with light weight wood roof or enclosures) derives from the desert landscape itself.

Left: Courtyards and pools provide shelter and coolness in the desert climate; Wright, his family, and his apprentices lived here in the wintertime. Above, top left: The bell tower provides an ancient function in a striking modern form. Above, bottom left: Steps and terraces echo the desert topography. Above, right: Taliesin's angular forms create stability on the desert soil, but Wright also uses them as an opportunity to explore new shapes in architecture.

Interior spaces blend the massive concrete piers rising from the desert soil with a light, tent-like wood roof structure.
Originally the ceiling was canvas, letting in translucent light. Elements like the built-in furniture and large fireplaces can be seen
in other Wright designs of the period, but the asymmetrical angles of the spaces show Wright exploring new territory.

The placement of windows shows light to be an important element of Wright's design composition.
Above, left: In the drafting room light is a functional element. Above right: Angled lines become a sculptural element around
the fireplace wall. Opposite: In a sitting area light reveals texture and shadow on the concrete and stone walls.

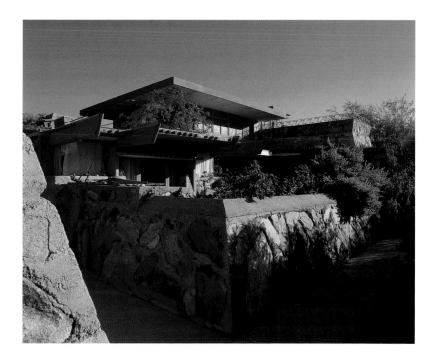

The Taliesin compound was a constant building project throughout Wright's life
and beyond. Besides his own quarters, his apprentices and colleagues also lived there.
Right: A wood trellis creates a long promenade along the main drafting room.

C. Leigh Stevens House

Auldbrass, Yemassee, South Carolina 1939 (1940)

Wright's resurgent Organic architecture asserted that any given site and client should generate a unique architecture—a fundamental principle quite different from Mies van der Rohe's conviction about a universal architecture that could, with minor adjustments, go anywhere. At Auldbrass in South Carolina, Wright develops a completely different design than those he did at Taliesin in the desert or Wingspread in the Midwest. Screened porches and wide eaves respond to the warm, humid climate.

Far right: The estate was an experimental farm testing tropical plants for export and includes barns, granaries, and shops, as well as the main house, guest cottages, pools, and terraces.

Above: The interior and its exposed wood structure carry on the same themes seen on the exterior.
Opposite: Languorous lines and eaves dripping with ornament demonstrate Wright's use of local conditions
and images for this particular design.

Left and above: Living room. The themes of Wright's earlier work continue in this
mid-century design. Spaces defined by the structure flow together; built-in and custom designed furniture
reinforce the lines of the architecture; the natural colors and textures of concrete floors, brick walls,
and wood ceilings create an opulent visual scene.

Though building on his previous work, Wright's later work pushes its spatial
and geometric complexity much further. Auldbrass's angled walls show Wright's adventurous
exploration of a new set of architectural forms and volumes.

C. Leigh Stevens intended Auldbrass to accommodate many visitors, so the house has many guest rooms. The structure's hexagonal geometry creates unusual room shapes, but the materials, the lighting sources, and the ornamental opportunities offered by the structure create rich, fully realized spaces.

Top, left: Clerestory window above dressing area. Below, left: Bathroom.
Above, right: Guest room.

Auldbrass was not completed as planned, but later owner Joel Silver completed and restored
the house according to the original plans. Above, left: Distinctive copper roof caps one of the farm buildings.
Above, right: Study fireplace. Right: Study.

Above: Interiors of guest cottages show a light and flexible structure.
Wright was intrigued by the possibilities of many different materials. Opposite: Guest cottages
are strewn among the native trees.

For all his sophistication, Wright was a farm boy from Wisconsin, as well.
Basic to his philosophy of life and architecture was the belief that even mundane and utilitarian buildings could
and should be thoughtful architecture, as seen in these barns, stables, dog runs, and hutches.

Stanley and Mildred Rosenbaum House

Florence, Alabama 1939

Quite distinct from the exotic individuality of Auldbrass is the Usonian house. This is a type of house meant to be affordable and useful for the average person, and Wright built dozens of them. The next several houses show both the similarities and the adaptations they expressed.

Right, top: To its suburban street, a Usonian house typically turns a mostly blank wall. Far right: To its back yard, the house opens up with glass walls. Right, bottom: Living room.

Above, left: The traditional dining room becomes a dining/living area in the Usonian house to save space and unite
the kitchen and living room. Above, right: Bedrooms are typically small, but use balanced light and warm materials. Opposite:
The living room focuses on a solid, brick fireplace. The entry is at the left, the kitchen and dining area at the right.

Goetsch-Winckler House

Okemos, Michigan 1939 (1940)

As Wright intended, the Usonian house garnered wide publicity. The simplicity (some said the starkness) of the architecture marked Wright's designs as ultramodern, especially in light of the popularity of the Colonial and the Ranch House style in the 1930s.

Right, top: A carport was typical in the Usonian house, even in colder climates. Right, bottom: the roof of the carport united it with the rest of the house's design. Far right: Living room.

The structure, space, and even furniture of a Usonian locked together like an intricate Chinese puzzle.
While Wright eliminated traditional ornamental molding to create a clean space, the brick and wood textures and
elegant proportions of the brick piers set his designs apart from the austere white planes of most
European Modernism of the era.

George Sturges House

Brentwood Heights, California 1939

On a steep site, a Usonian house could float, as the Sturges House appears to do. Right: Entry. Far right: A red brick foundation lifts the house, while cantilevered balconies create living space and impart a weightless appearance to the design.

Above: Vertical brick pylons and horizontal wood siding create a design that looks
much less like a traditional house than modern sculpture—an effect Wright cultivated as he sought
to redefine architecture. Left: Wide decks allow indoor and outdoor life to blend.

Above, left: Wright-designed chairs. Above, right: The fireplace supports one of the house's wood beams.
Right: Living room connects to deck.

Clarence Sondern House (Sondern-Adler)

Kansas City, Missouri 1939 (1948)

A local brick imparts a different tone to
this Kansas City Usonian house. Right, top:
Entry drive. Right, bottom, and far right:
Entry. Originally a much smaller, house, the
second owner invited Wright back to expand
this house.

Left: Wright uses varied floor and ceiling levels to shape the living room space.
Above, left: Kitchen. Above, right: Master bedroom.

Gregor and Elizabeth Affleck House

Bloomfield Hills, Michigan 1940

Like a piece of Modern art (and unlike most traditional houses), Wright's Usonians changed appearance from one side to the other.

Right, bottom: The side of the house away from the street is a broken composition of cubes and cantilevers. Right, top: Both sides can be seen from the end of the house. Far right: Sited on a slope, the Affleck house's broad roofs hover lightly over the ground.

Top, left: Interlocking brick and wood structure at entry. Top, right: Entry hall. Bottom left: Bathroom. Bottom, right: Bedroom. Far left: Polished concrete floors (marked with the regular module that organizes the entire house's geometry) would have been partly covered with rugs.

Lowell and Agnes Walter House

Quasqueton, Iowa 1945 (1948–1950)

In his last two decades, Wright's designs became even more fluid in responding to the needs of the client. His approach was clear: ignoring traditional forms and layouts, he used various geometries to choreograph a series of promenades, entries, conversation areas, intimate corners, views, and other household functions that seemed molded to the owner's requirements.

Right, top: Bedroom wing of house. Right, bottom: Skylights and clerestory windows cluster over the center of the living room to fill it with light. Far right: A broad terrace reaches out to lead the visitor to the front door, while the concrete roof shifts over to provide shelter from rain.

Top, left: Bedrooms have easy access to the outside. Top, right: The ceiling is as carefully designed as the rest of the room, letting in balanced light and providing ventilation. Bottom, left: Kitchen. Bottom right: Bedroom. Opposite: By leaving out alternate bricks, the house's structure also becomes ornament.

Top: Glass walls of the living room pavilion are sheltered by the wide eaves with distinctive upward-curved edges.
Bottom and right: A separate boathouse creates a living area at the river's edge. The house's motifs (brick walls, broad concrete roof) are repeated in a different arrangement to tie together the architecture and landscape.

Sara and Melvyn Smith House

Bloomfield Hills, Michigan 1946 (1950)

Many of Wright's clients for Usonian houses in the 1950s were educated people of fairly modest means who sought him out because of their deep attraction to his architecture and his philosophy. Sara and Melvyn Smith were schoolteachers, and helped to build their own house.

Right, top: Wright approved their selection of an irregular lot with a pond; it was both more challenging and less expensive.
Right, bottom: living room. Far right: Gate to back yard.

Above left: Dining area. Above right: Bathroom with wood walls. Opposite: Note the similarities between the living room view of the Smith fireplace and those in other Usonian houses. The brick, wood ceilings, and built-in furniture are repeated, but with different proportions and detailing. John Howe often designed the Usonians in Wright's office. Next page: In common with many suburban homes of the era, the Usonian house turned its back on the street to emphasize the private garden.

Herman T. Mossberg House

South Bend, Indiana 1946

A large two-story custom design, the Mossberg House's low gabled roofline and use of brick pillars echoes Wright's Susan Dana House from forty years before. The comparison illustrates how Wright simplified his forms and ornament over the years.

Right: garden view, with living room at left. Below: Stair is suspended on metal rods. Below, right: Dining area looks out onto back garden. Far right: The living room's window mullions develop the lines of the ceiling planes and trim.

Previous pages: Living room. Top: Bathroom. Bottom: Bedroom. Left: The two-story
front facade, topped with a gabled roof, appears remarkably traditional, though the simplicity
of detailing and the planting draping over the balcony are distinctive of Wright.

Mrs. Clinton Walker House

Carmel, California 1948

Few Wright house sites are as dramatic as that of the Walker House on Carmel Bay. The house's stone pedestal juts like the prow of a boat into the surf.

Right, top: Gate off of street. Right, bottom: Terrace. Far right: For an architect who drew inspiration from natural settings, this was a significant design balancing solidity and safety with a remarkable openness to the spectacular view.

Top: Living room windows step out on their steel frame. Openings for ventilation are on the steps parallel to the ground, moderating the stiff ocean breeze and leaving the view unobstructed. Bottom: Built-in seating makes efficient use of space in the living room of this relatively small house. Left: Only a few feet from the pounding waves, the living room becomes an observatory on the panoramic view.

Above, left: The house's parallelogram modules offered Wright opportunities for dramatic angles, as in the fireplace. Above, right: The small kitchen. Opposite: The house forms a small protected courtyard on the side away from the ocean breeze.

Above, left: A gallery hall to the bedrooms. Above, right: The bedroom incorporates the same stone walls used on the exterior to unify the design. Opposite: Local stone, copper roofs, and tinted concrete floors give the house its unique palette. Next page: The image of a light-weight steel pavilion perched on top of a solid stone foundation recurs in many Wright houses. It shows his intentional blending of advanced technology with nature.

Katherine and Maynard Buehler House

Orinda, California 1948

In the 1950s Wright usually avoided the
standard right angle as he explored the
spatial possibilities of different geometries.
These showed up in the sloping angles of
ceilings to the ornamental fantasias he
designed for window cut-outs.

Right: The living room flows into the dining
room. Far right: A long sheltered walk leads
the visitor to the entry.

Top, left: A gallery hall doubles as a library. Top, right: Entry walk.
Bottom, left: Each Wright house had a unique ornamental motif; here's a characteristic example.
Bottom, right: Terrace. Opposite: Dining room looking toward living room.

J. Willis Hughes House

Fountainhead, Jackson, Mississippi 1949

As he explored new architectural geometries, Wright also delighted in exploring various structural methods. The poured concrete walls of the Hughes House are marked by the long horizontal lines of the construction process; they complement the long low lines of the roofline.

Left: The complex geometries of this Wright house can be seen in the contrast of concrete walls and wood ceiling, of simple horizontal lines on the walls and repetitive wood trim on the ceiling; and in the angles of the ceiling, which allow moments for skylights and windows. Top, left: Entry hall. Top, right: Bedroom with varying levels. Bottom, left: Kitchen. Bottom, right: Bathroom.

Henry Neils House

Minneapolis, Minnesota 1949

In his radical campaign to remake the image of the American home, designs like the Neils House served admirably. Unlike the more extreme forms used by other Organic architects such as Bruce Goff and John Lautner, the gabled roof of this house was recognizable as that of a house. But the sharp prow-like roof lines, battered stone walls, and absence of traditional ornament made it ultramodern.

Right: Like many Wright houses, this one sits in a suburban setting. Far right: Living room wing.

Above, left: The living room fireplace continues the angled walls of the exterior, uniting inside and outside.

Above, right: Front door. Opposite: The living room is surrounded by glass and stone.

Above, left: Bedroom. Above, right: Kitchen. Right: Gallery to front door on right, bedrooms on left.

Anne and Eric Brown House

Parkwyn Village, Kalamazoo, Michigan 1949

The long, single-story Brown House takes the comfortable rambling form of the suburban ranch house, but its concrete structure and clean details mark it as a Wright house.

Right, top: Carport roof cantilevers out from the rest of the house. Right, bottom: Custom-sized concrete textile block building system gives the house a distinct set of proportions. Far right: This was one of the houses in a Wright-planned subdivision of Wright-designed houses in Kalamazoo, Michigan.

Where some Wright houses in later years relied on opulent ornament, the simpler Brown House plays the texture of the gray concrete block off against the warm reddish wood ceiling. Left, top: Opposite view of the living room, with fireplace at left. Left, bottom: Wright often combined the hallway with practical closet space. Right: bedroom repeats the folded planes of the living room's wood ceiling. Opposite: Living room.

Wilbur Pearce House

Bradbury, California 1950

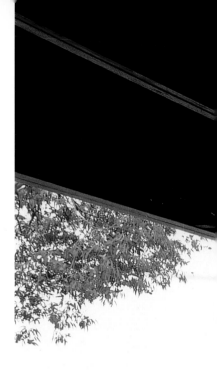

Curves were one of the most startling means Wright used to announce the modernity of his house designs. Like the Usonian house, his first effort in these hemicycle-shaped houses was designed for Katherine and Herbert Jacobs (see page 40). Also like the Usonian, they also became regularized in plan and form.

Top, right: The Pearce House sits on a hill overlooking the San Gabriel Valley. Bottom, right: The entry side appears squared off, with the car port on the left side. Far right: The view side features a long curving wall of glass in wood frames, accentuated by a wall and pond curving in the opposite direction.

Don and Mary Lou Schaberg House

Okemos, Michigan 1950

Top, right: As in his earliest Prairie houses, Wright integrates planters into the walls of the house. Bottom, right: The large single-family house reaches out in every direction, welcoming visitors at the handsome carport with its brick pylons. Far right: Wright's skill and sympathy in working with suburban houses on suburban sites is clear in this design for a large family.

Top: Bedroom window flows around the corner to let in the light and
view, while the plaster ceiling also continues uninterrupted from inside to outside.
Bottom: Gallery hallway to bedrooms. Left: Spacious living room.

R. Bradford and Ina Harper House

Saint Joseph, Michigan 1950

Top, right: Garden view. Bottom, right: Bedroom. Next pages: A high brick wall provides privacy while the even higher windows let in light. Far right: The living room ceiling sweeps upward to surround the living room with glass and permit a view of Lake Michigan. Next pages: A high brick wall provides privacy while the even higher windows let in light.

Robert and Gloria Berger House

San Anselmo, California 1950

The Bergers, clients with a young family, built this house over several years.

Right: Concrete and stone walls create flat terraces on the rolling site. Far right: Wright designed the house so that the Bergers could easily add on rooms to the right as their family grew.

Above, left: Original up-to-date kitchen oven. Above, right: Bedroom. Opposite: Built-in dining table links to kitchen.

William and Mary Palmer House

Ann Arbor, Michigan 1950

A design for a forested Midwestern lot prompts a different design.

Right: Stepped terraces and brick landscape walls create a frame for the house's main living room pavilion. Far right: Precast concrete blocks embedded in the brick wall offer one more opportunity for an ornamental touch, as does the copper light fixture.

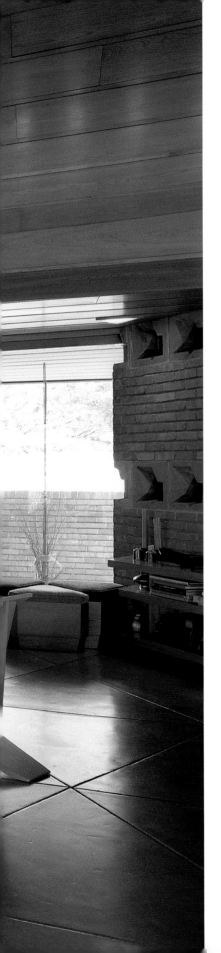

Top, left: French doors lead from living room to terrace. Top, right: Built-in dining table is part of the living room. Bottom, left: Bedroom. Bottom right: Kitchen workspace. Far left: This house's module of equilateral triangles (seen in the scored lines of the living room floor) brings a dynamic energy to its angled walls and ceilings. Next pages: Open carport at left, steps up to front door at right. Kitchen is in the central block with pierced windows.

Karl Staley House

North Madison, Ohio 1950

The plan of the Staley House is similar to those of the Usonian houses, but here Wright takes a distinct approach to the varied ceiling levels (evident in the low flat roofs and tall stone and wood volumes) to create a dramatic and original space.

Right, bottom: The high ceiling of the living room contrasts with a low soffit along the window wall at right. Far right: From left to right, the house includes a workshop, the car port, the tall stone kitchen space, and the master bedroom wing.

Above, left: Kitchen. Above right: Bedroom. Opposite: Always tying his designs back to nature,
Wright uses an irregular ashlar stone in this house's stone walls.

Russell and Ruth Kraus House

Kirkwood, Missouri 1950

Based on a parallelogram module, the Kraus House plan results in dramatic lines and prows that seem to hover over the landscape.

Top, right: Motor court nestles into ground. Carport is at left. Bottom, right: The studio's triangular roofline, at right, is balanced by the open terrace, at left. Far right: Front door.

Top, left: Entry to living room. Top, right: Kitchen with dining area on right.
Bottom, left: Master bedroom looking out to lanai. Bottom, right: Master bedroom with original parallelogram-shaped bed.
Opposite: Gallery leads from entry to bedroom. Living room is half way down on left.

Roland and Ronny Reisley House

Usonia Homes, Pleasantville, New York 1951

The Reisley House is one of three Wright houses designed for a planned community called Usonia, developed by Wright apprentice David Henken. Other houses were designed by Henken and other apprentices.

Top, right: Carport and front door. Bottom, right: Back terrace looking toward carport. Far right: The house lifts itself out of the sloping site. Stone walls and pylons increase the sense of the house growing out of the earth.

Above, left: Kitchen. Right, top: Dining area leads to terrace. Right, bottom: Bathroom. Opposite: Wright's use of a triangular module to lay out the walls and windows of the house creates an irregular shape for the living room. It demonstrates his "destruction" of the traditional box-shaped rooms; soft angles and walls of glass shift the emphasis to views, terraces, and conversation areas.

Gabrielle and Charlcey Austin House

Greenville, South Carolina 1951

In the Austin House Wright's contrasts strong stone and concrete walls with lighter-weight wood walls. The play of their textures, colors and solidity shapes the spaces.

Right, top: The wing with two bedrooms is at left, the living areas at right. Right, bottom: The uphill side of the house is lined with a wood wall punctured with cut-outs that allow light into the gallery hall. Far right: The large room echoes the slope of the hillside, tying the house to nature.

Above, left: Kitchen. Above, right: Master bedroom. Tall ceilings create dramatic spaces in small areas.
Opposite: Wright developed the rubblestone concrete wall in the Arizona desert, and used it widely in his later work
—though we see it here in South Carolina. Entry is to right of fireplace.

Nathan and Jeanne Rubin House

Canton, Ohio 1952

Right, top: The large hexagonal volume of the living spaces in the Rubin House at right dominates the smaller bedroom wing at left. Right, bottom: Living space wraps around a central fireplace at right. Far right: The high clerestory windows over the fireplace illuminate the center of the living room.

R. W. Lindholm House

Mäntylä, Cloquet, Minnesota 1952 (1956)

Right, top: Upswept roofs over the carport (left) and living room (right) give this house an ultramodern appearance. Right, bottom: Entry marker. Far right: The bold terrace wall makes the house grow from its rolling site; from his earliest Prairie houses a half century before, Wright sought to tie his houses to the land. Living room is at left, dining area at center, and bedroom wing at right.

Above: Some of Wright's later designs use simpler, plainer forms. The underlying geometry of this living room is complex, but the multi-textured character of the Usonian houses's walls, windows, and ceilings is absent. Opposite: Angled dining table looks toward kitchen and hall to bedrooms.

Jorgine Boomer House

Phoenix, Arizona 1952

A unique design among Wright's buildings, the Boomer House plan is based on three overlapping arrow-shaped volumes anchored by the tall stone chimney and staircase.

Right, top: Kitchen on first floor. Bottom: Desert stone walls wrap around the staircase. Right, bottom: Sitting room. Far right: The second story with two bedrooms rises over the entry in foreground. The upswept roof of the master bedroom at right shelters tall windows.

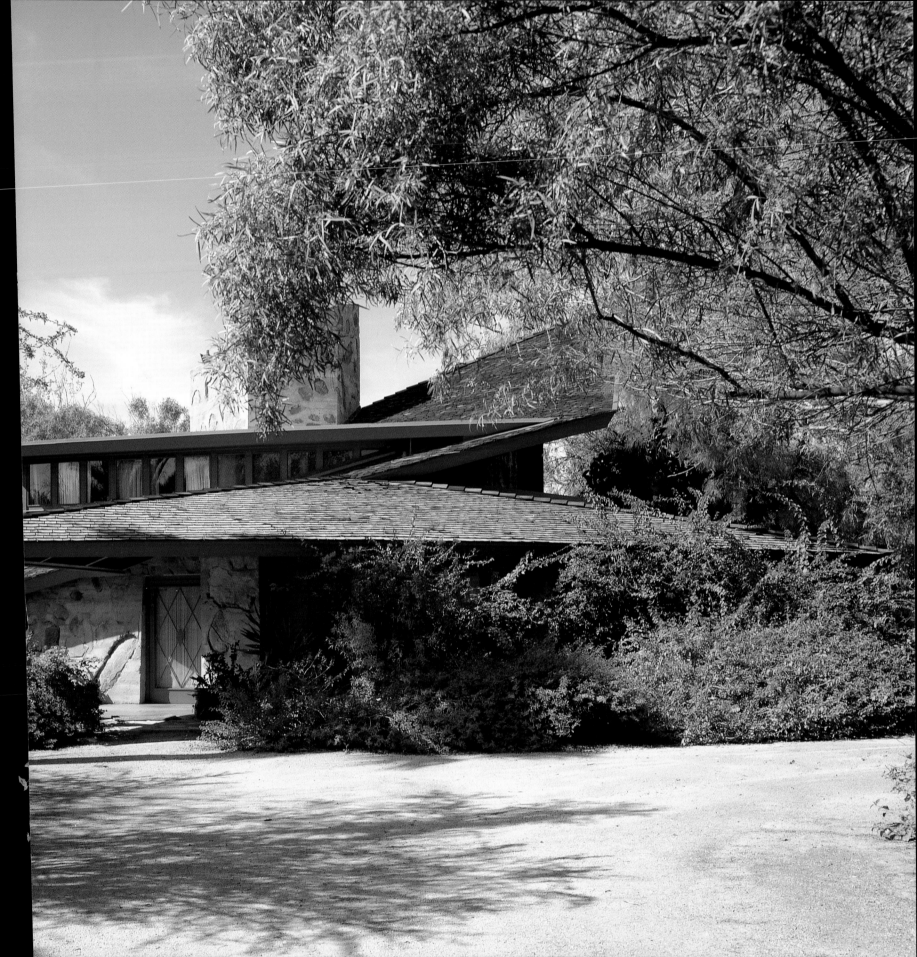

Andrew and Maude Cooke House

Virgina Beach, Virginia 1953 (1959)

The sleek lines of the long eave leading to the entry of the Cooke House, and the unconventional angles of walls and chimneys marking that entry, conveyed an extraordinarily modern image in the popular imagination of the times. That image was reinforced in the equally sleek curving glass wall that faces the living room (below).

Right: The large living room was intended for entertaining. Below right: master bedroom off the living room.

Harold Price Jr. House

Bartlesville, Oklahoma 1953

The Harold Price Jr. House is another large home combining simple lines and planes with warm textures and ornament.

Right: The living room balcony juts out over the sloping site; a hole in the cantilevered deck frames a fountain. Below, right: Entry hall. The front door is to the left, and the passage to the right leads to the living room. Far right: The accordion screen door seen here was designed at Taliesin.

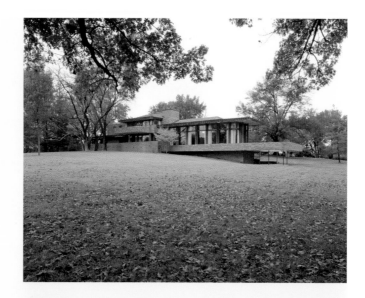

Above, left: Kitchen looking toward dining room. Above, right: Bathroom with original fixtures.
Opposite: Living room. Balcony at ceiling is off of master bedroom. Next pages: forecourt entry. Entry is at center,
bedrooms are in wing at right and on second floor. Living room is at far left.

William Thaxton House

Bunker Hill, Texas 1953

Wright pushes the envelope in this
ultramodern house.

Right, top: The composition is dynamic;
the tall angled block at right marks the
high-ceilinged kitchen, an anchor to the long
horizontal roofline reaching to the carport
at left. Right, bottom: The master bedroom
wall rises directly out of the swimming
pool. The two-story addition at left was not
designed by Wright. Far right: View from
living room to kitchen. Wright uses concrete
cinder blocks for the walls. They are
slightly set in as they rise to create a
horizontal pattern.

Gloria Bachman and Abraham Wilson House

Millstone, New Jersey 1954

Where the Thaxton House on the previous pages uses angular lines and sloping walls, the Bachman-Wilson House is straightforward and rectilinear.

Right: The broad concrete block wall facing the street is windowless, though a line of clerestory windows illuminate the upper living room. A bedroom balcony at left opens from one of the bedrooms. Far right: As in the Usonian houses, the living room here contrasts a solid wall on the left with a glassy wall on the right. Furniture is Wright-designed. Next pages: Garden side includes a master bedroom balcony at right.

Top: Balcony overlooking living room. Bottom: Bedroom on second floor.
Left: Dining table at right leads to the living room.

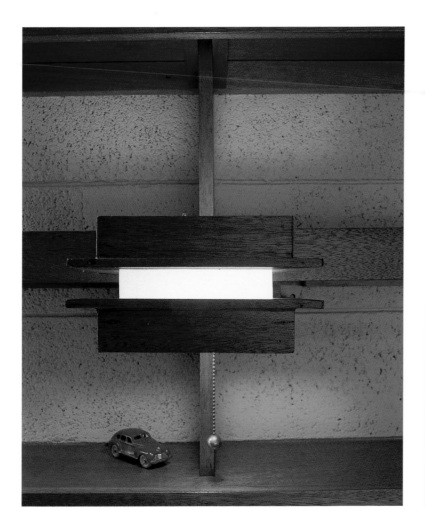

Above, left: Built-in wood light fixture against concrete block wall. Above, right: Bathroom with mahogany wood walls. Right: Kitchen.

Maurice and Margaret Greenberg House

Dousman, Wisconsin 1954

A repeated theme in Wright's later houses placed the kitchen (usually quite compact) in a tall space reflected on the exterior of the house as a short tower.

Right, top: The kitchen is seen at the right of the photograph. Right, bottom: Simple planar forms in plaster and brick were set at non-rectilinear angles. Far right: The house, situated on multiple levels, is poised dramatically over a steep slope.

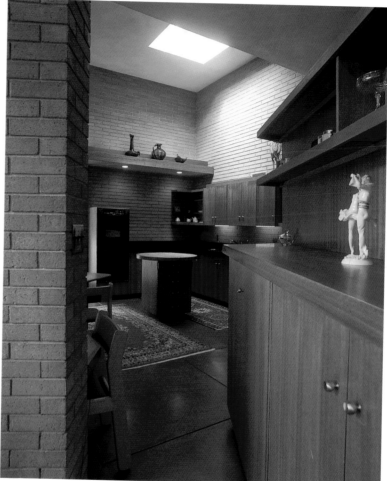

Little ornament is used in this house, in comparison with the repetitive coffering of the Usonian Automatic Tonkens House, or the scrollwork window cut outs of the Bachman-Wilson house. Above, left: Built-in sofa at corner of living room. Above, right: Kitchen. While most Wright houses in this period used a consistent module, three rectangular wings collided at arbitrary angles in this design, reflected in the kitchen's unusual angles. Opposite: Bold vertical brick masses contrast with strong horizontal ceiling planes. A warm tone unifies floor, walls and wood furnishings.

Harold Price Sr. House

Paradise Valley, Arizona 1954

Herbert Price Sr. gave Wright one of his greatest opportunities when he commissioned the Price Tower in Bartlesville, Oklahoma. For Price's winter house in Arizona, Wright created a compound of concrete block buildings strikingly different than Taliesin West.

Right: Ornamental door. Far right: Open air loggias and walkways made the most of the beautiful winter climate.

Above, left: Open entry with fountain. Above, right: The tall, flat-roofed central pavilion displays a startlingly different image than the ground-hugging, slope-roofed buildings at Taliesin West. Opposite: The living room used two modern industrial materials that Wright believed had aesthetic value for the modern age: concrete block walls (stepped out to create inverted columns) and Celotex ceilings, a manufactured acoustic tile set in a regular grid.

Cedric and Patricia Boulter House

Cincinnati, Ohio 1954 (1956)

Different sites and different materials demanded different architectural forms, Wright professed. While he did not always follow his own advice, a comparison of the Boulter House in Ohio with the Price House in Arizona on the previous pages shows his inventive abilities.

Right, top: A mostly blank wall on the northern, entry side presents a different face than the glass wall on the opposite side looking toward the view (bottom right). Far right: The mezzanine balcony creates low and tall spaces inside, and continues through the glass plane as a second story deck.

Above, left: Balcony to bedrooms overlooks living room. Wright had used such interlocking
spaces in the 1905 Hardy House in Racine, Wisconsin, and the 1923 Millard House in Pasadena, California.
Above, right: Bedroom. Opposite: Living room.

Gerald Tonkens House

Usonian Automatic, Amberley Village, Ohio 1954

Even in his eighth decade Wright was intrigued by exploring new mass-producible construction applications. He had worked with concrete in Unity Temple (1904) and the textile block houses in the 1920s; now he invented a system of fabricated coffered concrete blocks for a series of houses he called the Usonian Automatics, of which the Tonkens House is a prime example.

Right, top: The tall living room wing at right complemented the low bedroom wing at left. Right, bottom: The exterior blocks continued on the inside to create a honeycomb effect; the structure was also the integral textural ornament in this block system. Far right: Distinct blocks for flat walls, corner details, fascia trim and window blocks worked together in the design.

The Usonian Automatic system created an astonishingly unconventional yet unified appearance. Above, left: Dining area.
The block system was brilliantly conceived, but the insistent repetition of the concrete forms showed how Modern concepts could be taken
to an extreme. Above, right: Kitchen. Wood cabinetry softened the concrete structure. Opposite: Living room. Wright created
a variety of block sizes and proportions, and wove them together with his usual assured hand.

Though clothed in coffered block, the house's plan followed Wright's typical layout. Above, left: A long gallery,
lighted by high clerestories, leads to the bedrooms and includes built-in storage. Above, right: Bedroom. Opposite: bedroom.
Corner windows help to bring in balanced light, reflected on the ceiling.

Elizabeth and William Tracy House

Usonian Automatic, Normandy Park, Washington 1954

Each Usonian Automatic was a custom design, as was indeed the Tracy House.

Right: The concrete block system adapted well to the terraces, steps and walls that extended into the landscape, tying the architecture to nature. Opposite: The careful, at times fastidious, crafting of each Wright design can be seen in the precise placement of the window blocks, which turn the corner at the left of the front door.

While the severely planar Greenberg House expressed one aspect of Wright's later work, the Usonian Automatics echoed some of the lush, tapestry-like integration of structure and decoration seen in his Prairie houses. Top: Living room. Bottom: Living and dining areas flow together. As always, the hearth is a noticeable focal point to the house. Left: In these intriguing columns embedded with glass, Wright finds another way to blur the line between indoors and out.

Above left: Though the kitchen is small (a frequent criticism of Wright houses), a tall ceiling and high windows expand its apparent size. Above right: Bedroom. Opposite: Gallery from living room to bedrooms.

John Rayward House

Tirranna, New Canaan, Connecticut 1955

The Rayward House is a large estate based
on the single-story hemicycle form seen in
the Laurents, Pearce, and other houses.
Wright's colleague William Wesley Peters
designed later additions.

Right, top: Entry gate. Right, bottom: Curving
fascias knit together several masonry vertical
blocks, a Wrightian motif that makes the
building seem to be part of the natural
surroundings. Far right: Extensive artificial
ponds further tie the architecture to the
landscape.

Top, left: Living area. Top, right: Complementary curves of building and terrace walls impart a dynamic energy to the hemicycle designs. Bottom, left: Skylights inside living area continue as trellises outside, visually linking inside and outside. Bottom, right: Angled wood dentils add another layer of rich ornamental pattern to the design. Opposite: The long living space is marked by radial ceiling beams.

Additions by Wesley Peters, who led the Taliesin Fellowship office after Wright's death,
were made in 1964. Above, left: Greenhouse exterior. Above, right: Study. Bottom, left: Daughters' playhouse,
designed by Wright. Bottom, right: Office. Right: Greenhouse interior.

Above, left: Bathroom was also remodeled. Above, right: Landscape fountain. Opposite: Bedroom.

Harriet and Randall Fawcett House

Los Banos, California 1955 (1959–1961)

The Fawcett House represents many of Wright's most ultramodern and controversial ideas from his last two decades of work. Its forms are unconventional and inventive, its ornament is opulent, and it proudly—even arrogantly—contradicts the mainstream aesthetic of "less is more," which then dominated the architectural profession. That attitude led many to dismiss Wright as egotistical and eccentric.

Above, left: Entry court. Above, right: Bedroom wing is marked by upswept angular roof. Left: Wide eaves are punctured by elaborate copper ornament. Right: Wraparound living room is defined by a sloping ceiling, battered concrete block walls, and decorative clerestory windows.

H. and Dorothy Turkel House

Usonian Automatic, Detroit, Michigan 1955

The variety of spaces that could be
created with the Usonian Automatic system
is evident in the Turkel House.

Right: Exterior of living room wing.
Far right: The two-story living room uses
a large-scale grid.

Despite the heavy concrete structure, the house is light. Top: Living room at left, gallery at right.
Bottom: Second story balcony projects into living room space. Left: Gallery to kitchen wing. Next pages:
Garden side of the L-shaped house, which sits on a well-to-do suburban Detroit street.

Maximilian Hoffman House

Rye, New York 1955

The Hoffman House returns to the rectilinear asymmetry of early Wright designs, such as the 1907 Coonley House.

Right, top: The living room pavilion stands out from the rest of the house overlooking Long Island Sound. Right, bottom: Living and dining room. Far right: Entry car court. The wing visible through the porte-cochere was added in 1972 by Taliesin Associated Architects. Wright had also designed a 1954 auto showroom for Hoffman on Park Avenue in Manhattan.

Above, left: Ornamental wood trim along high windows between gallery and living room. Right, top: Dining area leading to sitting area. Right, bottom: Master bedroom. Opposite: Sitting area in addition.

Above: Stone wall with copper trellis ties pool terrace to the main house.
Right: low hipped roof pavilion with single story wings stretching out on either side
echo some of Wright's earliest Prairie designs.

Donald and Virginia Lovness House

Stillwater, Minnesota 1955

Wright's lifelong sensitivity to nature, to natural materials, and to architectural forms that abstract and blend them into profound pieces of design is evident in the Lovness House.

Right, top: The house is set in a Midwest forest similar to those of his native Wisconsin and adopted Illinois. Right, bottom: Living room fireplace uses rough hewn ashlar stone. Far right: Each horizontal and vertical element is carefully proportioned, arranged, and clad with wood or stone to create a composition that leads the eye and guides a visitor's approach.

Above left: Accordion screen door is used as an ornamental opportunity for a colorful geometric design.
Above, right: Dining area. Furniture is Wright-designed. Opposite: The Lovnesses were personal friends of Frank and
Olgivanna Wright, and shared their love of Asian art, seen in the statues in the living room.

A cottage designed for the site by Wright was finally built in 1976. Left, top:
Cottage living room. Left, bottom: Cottage kitchen. Right: The upswept roof, looking out to the lake,
is balanced by the stone pillar and the low wing extending back toward the woods.

Above, right: The compact cottage includes conversation areas, a fireplace, and other necessities
in an economic yet richly executed design. Above, left: View through open folding doors toward sleeping quarters.
Opposite: Folding doors, ornamented with gold leaf, open to the sleeping quarters.

Theodore and Bette Pappas House

Usonian Automatic, St. Louis, Missouri 1955

Right, top: Entry motor court.
Right, bottom: Front door. Far right: With
each rectilinear surface defined by a different
texture, this tall living room recalls Wright's
design for the 1923 Storer House, built with
textile concrete block.

Opposite: Dining area. Note the three steps up to the entry area at left; ceilings, walls, and
floors were all part of the palette of forms Wright manipulated to create a space. Above, left: Kitchen.
Above, right: Bedroom. Larger window blocks can be opened for ventilation.

Llewellyn and Elizabeth Wright House

Bethesda, Maryland 1956

In his later years Wright re-imagined the house in multiple ways: the jagged, crystalline Fawcett House, the intricately and compactly planned Usonian house, the honeycomb Usonian Automatics. The house he designed for his son Llewellyn offered yet another distinct vision: an ultramodern two-story design of interlocking curves.

Right: The front door is flanked on right by a tower with kitchen and bathroom. Far right: The terrace and pool continue theme of curves.

Top: Balcony off master bedroom. Bottom: Living room seen in opposite direction.
Opposite: Living room. The geometry of arcs unifies the space in the shapes of the space,
the furnishings, and the structure—a masterful coordination.

Top, left: Curving fascias reflect the forms of the projecting gallery-stairwell. Top, right: Staircase.
Bottom, left: Kitchen is contained in its own circular form. Bottom, right: Bedroom with balcony. Opposite: Pattern
of concrete block, shape of balustrade, placement of windows all play with the motif of curves.

Allen Friedman House

Bannockburn, Illinois 1956

The dominant horizontal roof, anchoring chimney pylon, and wide eaves of the Friedman House illustrate Wright's profound influence on, and knowledge of, the prototypical ranch house that spread throughout suburbia in the 1950s. Wright's suburban houses are nonetheless distinctive; this one is based on a consistent triangular module that creates sophisticated polygonal rooms, and is ornamented with custom designed copper fascias.

Right, top: Living room terrace looking toward gallery with clerestory windows. Right, bottom: Front door. Far right: Motor court.

Above: Built-in couch creates an inglenook by the fireplace, a motif in Wright houses since the 1890s. Here it is rendered in his later aesthetic: the large strokes of ceiling and structure are simplified and planar, though well arranged in unusual geometries. Built in ceiling lights and clerestory windows provide ornamental touches. Left: Living room.

Marshall Erdman Prefabricated Homes

1957 – 1961

Wright's long interest in mass-produced housing led to a series of pre-fabricated houses for developer Marshall Erdman. The concept of using assembly-line fabrication techniques to lower costs while creating a decent design was a central goal of many Modern architects; like most, Wright's scheme never had a major impact on the housing industry. Two models were built in a series of houses.

Right: The cube-like two-story James McBean House, Rochester, Minnesota (1957), featured a glass-enclosed two-story living room with a dining room bay. Far right: Examples of the linear model. Opposite, left to right, top to bottom: Eugene Van Tamelen House, Madison, Wisconsin, 1957; Frank Iber House, Stevens Point, Wisconsin, 1957; Arnold and Lora Jackson House, Madison, Wisconsin, 1957; Joseph Mollica House, Bayside, Wisconsin, 1958; Carl Post House, Barrington Hills, Illinois, 1957; Celeste and Socrates Zaferiou House, Blauvelt, New York, 1961.

James McBean House, Rochester, Minnesota, 1957. Above, left: View of living room and open stair from balcony of master bedroom. Above right: House is on three levels, including a basement, rare in Wright plans. Opposite: Two-story living room of the first cube-like Erdman model echoes the gridded windows of the Usonian Automatic houses. The structure combines concrete block with plywood panels.

Edward and Laura Jane LaFond House, St. Joseph, Minnesota, 1960. Top: The second linear ranch-style Erdman model included a carport at left, bedroom wing at right. Bottom: This model was designed to allow an open basement level if a sloping site allowed for it. Right: Though the prefab's plan was not as open as most Wright designs, it featured dropped soffits with indirect lighting over the dining area, and horizontal wood battens typical of Wright houses.

Edward and Laura Jane LaFond House, St. Joseph, Minnesota, 1960. Above, left: Gallery with built-in storage under clerestory windows is another common Wrightian feature, though the restraints of prefabrication appear to have limited Wright's design. Above, right: Kitchen. Right: Master bedroom features corner windows. Standardized prefabricated windows used in the Erdman houses noticeably alter the usual proportions of Wright designs.

Robert and Mary Walton House

Modesto, California 1957 (1961)

Right, top: Another example of Wright's simplification in some of his later houses. The projecting living room balances the long line of the bedroom wing along a terrace. Right, bottom: A corner of the large living room is articulated as a seating corner. Far right: Living room with entry at right, dining area and terrace beyond. The house is constructed of standard concrete block.

Next pages: Master bedroom wing at left, next to entry. Wright collects the vertical cubic forms over the kitchen and living room to balance the extraordinarily long bedroom wing at right; the house has six bedrooms plus a study and playroom.

Paul and Helen Olfelt House

Saint Louis Park, Minnesota 1958 (1960)

Right, top: The triangulated forms of the Olfelt House allow it to drape over the rolling site. It repeats the usual pattern of a distinct living room (left) and a bedroom wing (right) anchored by a tall, solid volume for the kitchen at the center. Right, bottom: Entry drive with carport at right and entry on a balcony next to it. Far right: Living room displays the angular space and forms of a triangular module design, in comparison with the rectilinear lines of the Walton House on the previous pages.

Above, left: Kitchen looking toward dining area. Above, right: Master bedroom repeats the living room's motif of a broad ceiling and prow-shaped window plane. Opposite: Asymmetric living room is shaped by the large ceiling plane that continues uninterrupted from inside to outside; the diamond-shaped window frames help to downplay the wall of enclosing glass by tying into the house's overall geometry.

George and Millie Ablin House

Bakersfield, California 1958 (1961)

The Ablin House stretches and exaggerates the prototypical suburban design seen in the Allen Friedman House.

Right, top: Three wings embrace the garden terrace. Right, bottom: Triangular tool shed with slanting walls anchors the end of the carport in a sharply chiseled composition. The tall kitchen tower perforated with glass-filled concrete blocks marks the front entry. Far right: Entry gate announces the house's geometries.

Above left: Perforated concrete block create a screen wall for the kitchen. Right, top: Triangular swimming pool
repeats the house's module at a large scale. Right, bottom: Master bedroom. Opposite: Living room ceiling sweeps dramatically from
a low eave to a high prow. The window wall is treated as a light angled screen. Next page: Living room with terrace.

Don Stromquist House

Bountiful, Utah 1958 (1963)

Right: Shutters reiterate the plan's complexity in its ornamental filigree. Far right: Complex geometry of sloping, angular roof on top of a plan based on the parallelogram creates this distinctive facade.

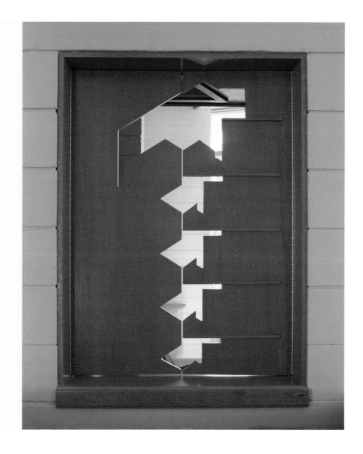

Left, top: Living room window walls have the feel of free-standing screens, a concept used in the Hanna house.
Right, top: Front door seen past living room fireplace. Left, bottom: Master bedroom terrace. Opposite: Front door at carport.
Door frame reflects the house's angled geometry.

Seth Condon Peterson Cottage

Lake Delton, Wisconsin 1958 (1959)

One of Wright's smallest houses, this design uses a few walls to shape an elegant variety of useful spaces. Wright's later buildings are definitively modern in their use of clean lines and new materials. But their primary focus is their link with nature. In this simple yet rich design, his choice of irregular stonework that abstracts natural rock outcroppings, and his complex arrangement of diagonal, vertical, and horizontal forms, demonstrate how he learned from the opulent variety of the natural world.

Right: As is typical, the stone terrace walls allow the house to appear as if it is rising out of the native earth. Far right: Upswept roof on a light wood frame shelters the living space. Stone tower marks the bathroom and kitchen, with the bedroom in the low wing at right.

Above, left: Living area is focused on fireplace. Modernistic Wright furniture
contrasts with the natural stone walls. Bedroom is at left of fireplace. Above, right: bedroom.
Opposite: Entry leads to dining area, with living room beyond.

Above: Rich organic designs at top of window wall reflect the patterns of flowers,
leaves, and branches in the environment—one way in which his designs draw on and link with nature.
Right: In its lines and materials, the house reflects nature.

HOUSE LIST

Edited by Alan Hess

This list includes the original client's name, and the earliest known date when a project was first conceived, commissioned, or designed, as confirmed by The Frank Lloyd Wright Foundation. This order is intended to roughly approximate the evolution of Wright's design ideas as they unfolded on his drafting table.

1933

Malcolm Willey House
Minneapolis, Minnesota

1935

Liliane and Edgar J. Kaufmann House (Fallingwater)
Mill Run, Pennsylvania

Abby Roberts House (Deertrack)
Marquette, Michigan

1936

Herbert and Katherine Jacobs House I (1937)
Madison, Wisconsin

Jean and Paul Hanna House
(Honeycomb House)
Palo Alto, California

1937

Herbert Johnson House
(Wingspread)
Wind Point, Wisconsin

Ben Rebhuhn House
Great Neck Estates, New York

1938

Taliesin West
Scottsdale, Arizona

Suntop Homes
Ardmore, Pennsylvania

Charles L. Manson House
Wausau, Wisconsin

John C. Pew House (1940)
Shorewood Hills, Wisconsin

Rose Pauson House (Shiprock)
Phoenix, Arizona / demolished

1939

C. Leigh Stevens House
(Auldbrass) (1940)
Yemassee, South Carolina

Sidney Bazett House
Hillsborough, California

Andrew Armstrong House
Ogden Dunes, Indiana

Lloyd Lewis House
Libertyville, Illinois

Stanley and Mildred Rosenbaum House
Florence, Alabama

Loren B. Pope House (1941)
(Pope-Leighey House)
Falls Church, Virginia

Goetsch-Winckler House (1940)
Okemos, Michigan

Joseph Euchtman House
Baltimore, Maryland

Bernard Schwartz House
Two Rivers, Wisconsin

George Sturges House
Brentwood Heights, California

Clarence Sondern House
(Sondern-Adler) (1948)
Kansas City, Missouri

1940

Gregor and Elizabeth Affleck House
Bloomfield Hills, Michigan

Arch Oboler House
Malibu, California

Theodore Baird House (1941)
Amherst, Massachusetts

James B. Christie House
Bernardsville, New Jersey

1941

Stuart Richardson House (1951)
Glen Ridge, New Jersey

Carlton and Margaret Wall House (Snowflake)
Plymouth, Michigan

1944

Herbert and Katherine Jacobs House II (1946–1948)
Middleton, Wisconsin

1945

Lowell and Agnes Walter House
(1948–1950)
Quasqueton, Iowa

Arnold Friedman House
(The Fir Tree)
Pecos, New Mexico

1946

Sara and Melvyn Smith House (1950)
Bloomfield Hills, Michigan

Douglas and Jackie Grant House (1951)
Cedar Rapids, Iowa

Chauncey and Johanna Griggs House
Tacoma, Washington

Alvin Miller House
Charles City, Iowa

Amy Alpaugh House
Northport, Michigan

Herman T. Mossberg House
South Bend, Indiana

1947

A. H. Bulbulian House
Rochester, Minnesota

Carroll Alsop House
Oskaloosa, Iowa

Jack Lamberson House
Oskaloosa, Iowas

Charles Weltzheimer House
Oberlin, Ohio

1948

David and Christine Weisblat House
Galesburg, Michigan
Galesburg Country Homes

Eric and Pat Pratt House
Galesburg, Michigan
Galesburg Country Homes

Samuel Eppstein House
Galesburg, Michigan
Galesburg Country Homes

Lillian and Curtis Meyer House
Galesburg, Michigan
Galesburg Country Homes

Robert Levin House
Kalamazoo, Michigan
Parkwyn Village

Mrs. Clinton Walker House
Carmel, California

Albert Adelman House
Fox Point, Wisconsin

Katherine and Maynard Buehler House
Orinda, California

Erling and Katherine Brauner House (1949)
Okemos, Michigan

Sol Friedman House
Pleasantville, New York
Usonia Homes

1949

J. Willis Hughes House
(Fountainhead)
Jackson, Mississippi

James and Dolores Edwards House
Okemos, Michigan

Henry Neils House
Minneapolis, Minnesota

Howard and Helen Anthony House
Benton Harbor, Michigan

Edward Serlin House
Pleasantville, New York
Usonia Homes

Helen and Ward McCartney House
Kalamazoo, Michigan
Parkwyn Village

Anne and Eric Brown House
Kalamazoo, Michigan
Parkwyn Village

Kenneth and Phyllis Laurent House
Rockford, Illinois

1950

Robert D. Winn House
Kalamazoo, Michigan
Parkwyn Village

Wilbur Pearce House
Bradbury, California

David Wright House
Phoenix, Arizona

John Haynes House
Fort Wayne, Indiana

Richard and Madelyn Davis House
Marion, Indiana

J. A. and Muriel Sweeton House
Cherry Hill, New Hersey

Raymond Carlson House
Phoenix, Arizona

John Carr House
Glenview, Illinois

Don and Mary Lou Schaberg House
Okemos, Michigan

R. Bradford and Ina Harper House
Saint Joseph, Michigan

Robert and Gloria Berger House
San Anselmo, California

Arthur Mathews House
Atherton, California

William and Mary Palmer House
Ann Arbor, Michigan

Isadore and Lucille Zimmerman House (1952)
Manchester, New Hampshire

Robert and Elizabeth Muirhead House (1951)
Plato Center, Illinois

Karl Staley House
North Madison, Ohio

S. P. Elam House
Austin, Minnesota

Berenice and Richard Smith House
Jefferson, Wisconsin

John Gillin House (1955–1958)
Dallas, Texas

Seamour and Gerte Shavin House
Chattanooga, Tennessee

Russell and Ruth Kraus House
Kirkwood, Missouri

Welbie Fuller House
Pass Christian, Mississippi
destroyed 1969

1951

Thomas Keys House
Rochester, Minnesota

Roland and Ronny Reisley House
Pleasantville, New York
Usonia Homes

Charles Glore House
Lake Forest, Illinois

Margaret and Patrick Kinney House
Lancaster, Wisconsin

Benjamin Adelman House
Phoenix, Arizona
Usonian Automatic

Gabrielle and Charlcey Austin House
Greenville, South Carolina

A. K. Chahroudi Cottage
Lake Mahopac, New York

Arthur Pieper House
Paradise Valley, Arizona
Usonian Automatic

1952

Nathan and Jeanne Rubin House
Canton, Ohio

Ray Brandes House
Issaquah, Washington

Quintin and Ruth Blair House
Cody, Wyoming

Archie and Patricia Teater Studio
Bliss, Idaho

R. W. Lindholm House
(Mäntylä) (1956)
Cloquet, Minnesota

Frank Sander House
(Springbough)
Stamford, Connecticut

Price Tower (1953–1956)
Bartlesville, Oklahoma

Clifton and George Lewis House
(Spring House)
Tallahassee, Florida

Jorgine Boomer House
Phoenix, Arizona

Louis Penfield House
Willoughby Hills, Ohio

1953

Louis Marden House
McLean, Virginia

Andrew and Maude Cooke House (1959)
Virgina Beach, Virginia

John and Syd Dobkins House
Canton, Ohio

Harold Price Jr. House
Bartlesville, Oklahoma

Lewis Goddard House
Plymouth, Michigan

William Thaxton House
Bunker Hill, Texas

1954

Gloria Bachman and Abraham Wilson House
Millstone, New Jersey

Karen Johnson (Keland) House
Racine, Wisconsin

Alice and Ellis Feiman House (1955)
Canton, Ohio

Maurice and Margaret Greenberg House
Dousman, Wisconsin

E. Clarke Arnold House
Columbus, Wisconsin

John and Catherine Christian House (1956)
West Lafayette, Indiana

Louis Fredrick House
Barrington Hills, Illinois

I. N. Hagan House
Chalkhill, Pennsylvania

Harold Price Sr. House
Paradise Valley, Arizona

Cedric and Patricia Boulter House (1956)
Cincinnati, Ohio

Gerald Tonkens House
Amberley Village, Ohio
Usonian Automatic

Elizabeth and William Tracy House (1960)
Normandy Park, Washington
Usonian Automatic

1955

John Rayward House (Tirranna)
New Canaan, Connecticut

Harriet and Randall Fawcett House (1959–1961)
Los Banos, California

Toufic Kalil House
Manchester, New Hampshire
Usonian Automatic

H. And Dorothy Turkel House
Detroit, Michigan
Usonian Automatic

Maximilian Hoffman House
Rye, New York

Donald and Virginia Lovness House
Stillwater, Minnesota

Theodore and Bette Pappas House (1964)
St. Louis, Missouri
Usonian Automatic

Robert Sunday House (1963)
Marshalltown, Iowa

1956

Llewellyn and Elizabeth Wright House
Bethesda, Maryland

Paul and Ida Trier House (1960)
Johnston, Iowa

Dudley Spencer House
Wilmington, Delaware

Allen Friedman House (1960)
Bannockburn, Illinois

Conrad Edward and Evelyn Gordon House (1964)
Wilsonville, Oregon

Julia and Duey Wright House (1959)
Wausau, Wisconsin

1957

Frank and Eloise Bott House (1963)
Kansas City, Missouri

Eugene Van Tamelen House
Madison, Wisconsin
Marshall Erdman Prefabricated Homes

Arnold and Lora Jackson House
Madison, Wisconsin
Marshall Erdman Prefabricated Homes

Elizabeth and Don Duncan House
Lisle, Illinois
Marshall Erdman Prefabricated Homes

Frank Iber House
Stevens Point, Wisconsin
Marshall Erdman Prefabricated Homes

Carl Post House
Barrington Hills, Illinois
Marshall Erdman Prefabricated Homes

James McBean House
Rochester, Minnesota
Marshall Erdman Prefabricated Homes

Mary Ellen and Walter Rudin House
Madison, Wisconsin
Marshall Erdman Prefabricated Homes

Robert and Mary Walton House (1961)
Modesto, California

Dorothy Ann and Sterling Kinney House (1961)
Amarillo, Texas

William Boswell House (1961)
Indian Hill, Ohio

Carl Schultz House (1959)
Saint Joseph, Michigan

1958

Paul and Helen Olfelt House (1960)
Saint Louis Park, Minnesota

George and Millie Ablin House (1961)
Bakersfield, California

Don Stromquist House (1963)
Bountiful, Utah

Seth Condon Peterson Cottage (1959)
Lake Delton, Wisconsin

Joseph Mollica House
Bayside, Wisconsin
Marshall Erdman Prefabricated Homes

1959

William and Catherine Cass House
Staten Island, New York
Marshall Erdman Prefabricated Homes

Aime and Norman Lykes House (1966–1968)
Phoenix, Arizona

1960

Edward and Laura Jane LaFond House
St. Joseph, Minnesota
Marshall Erdman Prefabricated Homes

1961

Celeste and Socrates Zaferiou House
Blauvelt, New York
Marshall Erdman Prefabricated Homes

BIBLIOGRAPHY

Amin, Kamal. *Reflections from the Shining Brow: My Years with Frank Lloyd Wright and Olgivanna Lazovich*. Santa Barbara: Fithian Press, 2004.

Barry, Joseph. *The House Beautiful Treasury of Contemporary American Homes*. New York: Hawthorn Books, Inc, Publisher, 1958.

Dunham, Judith. *Details of Frank Lloyd Wright: The California Work, 1909–1974*. San Francisco: Chronicle Books, 1994.

Friedland, Roger and Harold Zellman. *The Fellowship: The Untold Story of Frank Lloyd Wright & The Taliesin Fellowship*. New York: HarperCollins Publishers, 2006.

Germany, Lisa. *Harwell Hamilton Harris*. Berkeley: University of California Press, 2000.

Gordon, Elizabeth. "Your Legacy from Frank Lloyd Wright: A Richer Way of Life. *House Beautiful* (October 1959), pp. 207-211.

Hess, Alan. *The Architecture of John Lautner*. New York: Rizzoli International Publications, 1999.

Hitchcock, Henry-Russell. "An Eastern Critic Looks at Western Architecture." *California Arts and Architecture* (December 1940), pp. 21-23, 40.

Izzo, Alberto and Camillo Gubitosi. *Frank Lloyd Wright: Drawings 1887–1959*. London: Academy Editions, 1977.

Jacobs, Herbert with Katherine Jacobs. *Building with Frank Lloyd Wright: An Illustrated Memoir*. San Francisco: Chronicle Books, 1978.

Levine, Neil. *The Architecture of Frank Lloyd Wright*. Princeton: Princeton University Press: 1996.

Pfeiffer, Bruce Brooks and Gerald Nordland, eds. *Frank Lloyd Wright: In the Realm of Ideas*. Carbondale, IL: Southern Illinois University Press, 1988.

Peisch, Mark L. *The Chicago School of Architecture: Early Followers of Sullivan and Wright*. New York: Random House, 1964.

Scully, Vincent. *Frank Lloyd Wright*. New York: George Braziller, 1960.

Secrest, Meryle. *Frank Lloyd Wright: A Biography*. New York: Alfred A. Knopf, 1992.

Smith, Elizabeth A. T., ed. *Blueprints for Modern Living: History and Legacy of the Case Study Houses*. Cambridge: MIT Press, 1989.

Smith, Kathryn. *Frank Lloyd Wright: Hollyhock House and Olive Hill*. New York: Rizzoli International Publications, 1992.

Storrer, William Allin. *The Frank Lloyd Wright Companion*. Chicago: The University of Chicago Press, 1993.

Storrer, William Allin. *The Architecture of Frank Lloyd Wright: A Complete Catalog*. Chicago: University of Chicago Press, 2002.

Tafel, Edgar Tafel. *About Wright: an album of recollections by those who knew Frank Lloyd Wright*. New York: John Wiley and Sons, Inc., 1993.

Tafel, Edgar. *Apprentice to Genius: Years with Frank Lloyd Wright*. New York: McGraw-Hill Book Co.,1979, p. 122.

Twombley, Robert C. *Frank Lloyd Wright: His Life and His Architecture*. New York: John Wiley and Sons, Inc.,1979.

Weintraub, Alan. *Lloyd Wright: The Architecture of Frank Lloyd Wright, Jr.* London: Thames & Hudson, 1998.

ENDNOTES

Frank Lloyd Wright: Mid-Century Modern
By Alan Hess

1. The 1954 Beth Shalom Synagogue is based on a 1926 Steel Cathedral. The 1952 Price Tower was designed in 1929 for St. Mark's Apartments in New York. The teepee-form 1945 Arnold Friedman and 1950 Richard Davis houses are based on designs for Tahoe Cabins in 1923 and the Nakoma Country Club from 1924.

2. Bruce Brooks Pfeiffer and Gerald Nordland, eds. *Frank Lloyd Wright: In the Realm of Ideas* (Carbondale, IL: Southern Illinois University Press, 1988), p. 91.

3. Kathryn Smith. *Frank Lloyd Wright: Hollyhock House and Olive Hill* (New York: Rizzoli International Publications, 1992), p. 82.

4. William Allin Storrer. *The Frank Lloyd Wright Companion* (Chicago: The University of Chicago Press), p. 250.

5. Roger Friedland and Harold Zellman. *The Fellowship: The Untold Story of Frank Lloyd Wright & The Taliesin Fellowship* (New York: HarperCollins Publishers, 2006), p. 150.

6. Wright had designed a Hollywood house named "Aladdin" for John Gillin in 1956.

7. Wright never used this particular detail, but his student John Lautner incorporated it as the "infinity edge" swimming pool in the Silvertop House (1959) for Ken Reiner. The detail has since become a popular luxury design item.

8. Alberto Izzo and Camillo Gubitosi. *Frank Lloyd Wright: Drawings 1887–1959* (London: Academy Editions, 1977), drawing number 186.

9. Friedland and Zellman, p. 503.

10. Izzo and Gubitosi, drawing number 71.

11. Ibid., drawing number 132.

Frank Lloyd Wright and World War II, 1939–45
By John Zukowsky

1. I first presented some of the observations about Frank Lloyd Wright and other American architects, in relation to isolationism in the early years of World War II, and the importance of *A Taliesen Square-Paper* from 1941 in documenting this, in a symposium on Chicago at the University of Hamburg, June 8–10, 2000.

2. See various references to his criticism of how European modernists misrepresented him, especially as regards an unpublished essay for his 1940 Museum of Modern Art exhibition in *The Show to End all Shows: Frank Lloyd Wright and The Museum of Modern Art, 1940*, ed. Peter Reed and William Kaizen (Museum of Modern Art: New York, 2004).

3. W. David Lewis, *Eddie Rickenbacker: An American Hero in the Twentieth Century* (Johns Hopkins University Press: Baltimore, 2005), especially pp. 364, 383-84, 386.

4. For American architects during the war, see my introductory essay in *1945 Creativity and Crisis: Chicago Architecture and Design of the World War II Era* (Chicago: exhibition catalog at The Art Institute of Chicago: Chicago, 2005). For Wright during the war, see: Brendan Gill, *Many Masks: A Life of Frank Lloyd Wright* (Da Capo Press: New York, 1987), p.p 415-18. ; Donald Leslie Johnson, *The Fountainheads: Wright, Rand, the FBI, and Hollywood* (McFarland: Jefferson, N.C., 2005), particularly pp. 89-97; Roger Friedland and Harold Zellman, *The Fellowship: The Untold Story of Frank Lloyd Wright and the Taliesin Fellowship* (Regan: New York, 2006), pp. 348-49, 361-63, and 367-73, this last including a number of unrealistic proposals that Wright made to various government officials efforts to obtain wartime jobs.

Exuberant Fifties: Wright and the Guggenheim
By Monica Ramírez Montagut

1. There was a moratorium on materials and technological innovations which were set aside exclusively for the military.

2. Manfredo Tafuri and Francesco Dal Co considered Saarinen's architecture a symptom of a crisis in Modern architecture. Eeva-Liisa Pelkonen and Donald Albrecht, "Introduction" in *Eero Saarinen, Shaping the Future* (New Haven: Yale University Press, 2006) p. 7.

3. The positioning of Wright on the margins of the modern movement was early on evident at the MoMA's 1932 exhibition *Modern Architecture, International Exhibition*, where his work was not presented. Regardless of Wright's constant efforts to be included within the "Modern architecture" category, the recognition of many of his contemporary peers, and most importantly common searches in terms of optimism for standardized systems, encouragement of interaction between industry, architecture and the visual arts, the belief in the symbolic potential of the geometry (for example, both Wright and Le Corbusier, were exposed in their childhood to the Froebel blocks teaching method), the expression of the function and structure of the building, and engaging the dynamic potential of the open plan, his work is still today not generally identified with the quintessential Modern architecture.

4. After years of waiting for the high cost of construction materials caused by war demand to go down, Solomon Guggenheim had recently died and Hilla Rebay, the museum's first director and the one responsible for Wright's introduction to the project, was becoming less involved; it ultimately prompted her resignation in 1953.

5. The project was first originated in 1929 for the St. Marks in the Bouwerie in New York.

6. Artists of the time including Calvin Albert, Milton Avery, Will Barnet, Paul Bodin, Henry Botkin, Byron Browne, Herman Cherry, George Constant, William de Kooning, Herbert Ferber, Adolph Gottlieb, Philip Guston, Franz Kline, Seymour Lipton, Sally Michel, George L. F. Morris, Robert Motherwell, Charles Shucker, John Sennhauser, Leon P. Smith, and Jack Tworkov sensed the untraditionally Modern space for art display would not establish the best relationship between art and architecture and in 1957 wrote an open letter to officially complain. In *Frank Lloyd Wright: The Guggenheim Correspondence* (Carbondale, IL: Southern Illinois University Press), p. 242.

7. *Frank Lloyd Wright: The Guggenheim Correspondence* (Carbondale, IL: Southern Illinois University press), p. 234.

8. Wright died seven months before the opening of the museum.

9. Wright considered stark white would become a foreground instead of background on a museum wall and thus proposed an ivory color which was capable of receiving luminosity; ivory, current color at the museum, would self-efface instead of compete with the art works' compositions.

10. Gloria Koening. *Charles and Ray Eames* (Germany: Taschen GmbH, 2005), p. 8.

11. Wright tended to compliment Eliel's accomplishments of a total work of art, architecture, and design on such a large scale project such as the Cranbrook campus, however, he also recognized himself as America's most prominent architect.

12. From: "Lecture delivered at Dickinson College, Carlisle, Pennsylvania, on December 1, 1959" in *Eero Saarinen, Shaping the Future*. Edited by Eeva-Liisa Pelkonen and Donald Albrecht (New Haven: Yale University Press, 2006), p. 347.

13. Stern, Robert A. M., Thomas Mellins, and David Fishman, eds. *New York 1960: Architecture and Urbanism Between the Second World War and the Bicentennial* (New York: The Monacelli Press, 1995), p. 815.

14. Bruno Zevi described Saarinen as a Manerist architect who was contributing to the decline of Modern architecture and distancing it from the premise "form follows function." This appears in the introduction to *Eero Saarinen, Shaping the Future*. Edited by Eeva-Liisa Pelkonen and Donald Albrecht (New Haven: Yale University Press, 2006), p. 4.

15. Roeder and New York Daily News, quoted in Peter Blake: "The Guggenheim: Museum or Monument?" *Architectural Forum 3*

INDEX

Note: Page numbers in *italics* refer to photographs